Who Is Our Church?

Who Is Our Church?

Imagining Congregational Identity

Janet R. Cawley

THE
ALBAN
INSTITUTE

Herndon, Virginia
www.alban.org

The Alban Institute
2121 Cooperative Way, Suite 100
Herndon, VA 20171

Cover design by Adele Robey, Phoenix Graphics.

Library of Congress Cataloging-in-Publication Data

Cawley, Janet R.
  Who is our church? : imagining congregational identity / Janet
R. Cawley.
    p. cm.
  Includes bibliographical references.
  ISBN-13: 978-1-56699-321-0
  ISBN-10: 1-56699-321-0
  1. Church management. 2. Social surveys. 3. Group identity. I.
Title.

  BV652.4.C39 2006
  250—dc22

                              2006004760

12 11 10 9 8 7 6   VG   1 2 3 4 5 6 7 8

For Sallie McFague

Contents

Foreword

Life in congregations seems more complicated with every passing year. More and more is demanded of church leaders—lay or ordained, paid or volunteer. In fact, I sometimes marvel that people still offer themselves for these roles and that so many still find deep satisfaction in them. As the Peace Corps poster used to say, this is "the toughest job you'll ever love!"

Part of the challenge is that an individual congregation is more directly responsible than ever before to discern its own particular calling—that sense of purpose and direction that is unique to the church's history and personality, to its community setting and its wider cultural context. This heightened responsibility can be exhilarating, but it can also seem overwhelming in the face of alarming world events, rapid change in local communities, painful stresses within denominational systems, and the wide range of expectations that members and visitors bring with them every week.

When a congregation asks, "How might we search for our distinctive calling?" the answer it receives may seem as daunting as the question itself. Theories and research studies help, but there are so many of them, and they don't all agree! Planning or visioning processes may help, but some of them are quite complicated—even draining—and leadership energy may be in short supply. Outside consultants can be useful, but how do we choose one, and what will they do, and can we afford their assistance?

Cutting through much of this complexity, Janet Cawley has offered one option for exploring identity and call: helping people develop and interact with an image of their congregation as a specific "person." Through her many stories from her twenty years of experimentation with the method, primarily in her role as an interim minister, she demonstrates an approach that is within the reach of congregations of many sizes, in many places, facing many different circumstances. This process for exploring congregational identity and direction resembles and complements many other techniques, but it has about it a special wisdom and simplicity and spiritual depth that will make it a "new classic" among congregational development interventions.

What characteristics of the process would lead me to this conclusion? First, the method is rooted in a biblical and theological affirmation, offered explicitly and implicitly to the congregation throughout the process: "You—knit together as a congregation—are the body of Christ." As often as we hear those words, it still feels a little shocking to apply them to any one, specific congregation. After all, when we see the church close up, when we examine its life at that level of local detail, we can't possibly miss the limitations, the foibles, and the sometimes disastrous errors and omissions of the People of God. Cawley's process goes right out on the limb with St. Paul to affirm—without sentimentality—the deeper reality hidden underneath the current mess or confusion or boredom. "You *are* the body of Christ."

Second, this method builds an imaginative frame that is accessible to people of different cultures, backgrounds, and ages. Embodiment is the experience we share in common with every human being. It is also the thing we share in common with Jesus and with the congregation as a social and spiritual organism. So the project of imagining a body to represent this particular congregation is both child-like and powerful.

Third, this is a method best administered by leaders serving *inside* the congregation, rather than by an outside facilitator. Those leaders will need help preparing themselves for the work, but the book is a wonderful start, and additional coaching might come from a variety of sources. It won't be long, I suspect, before many of the people who come alongside congregations as insightful companions— such as denominational staff, interim ministers, church consultants, and coaches—will have gained first-hand experience with this method and be able to help others apply it appropriately. (All of us who may try this method should take careful note of the limitations Cawley has identified. It is not appropriate too early in a new pastorate, in the midst of high-level conflict or immediately after a trauma, or too soon after a merger or amalgamation of congregations.)

For all these reasons, Cawley's work is likely to zing around the continent and around the globe in practitioners' kit-bags, alongside other elegantly simple tools like

African Bible study or congregational life-cycle curves. So, read the book with care. Enjoy the stories. Attend to the disciplines and caveats the author provides as you prepare for each specific event.

Then, enjoy the ride. To borrow the words of W. H. Auden, you will be following Christ through the "land of Unlikeness"; you will be loving Christ "in the World of the Flesh"; and you will most probably come to a "great city that has expected your return for years."

Alice Mann

Acknowledgments

This book could not exist without the congregations I have been privileged to minister with over the last 30 years. All of them, sharing their struggles to be the body of Christ in their place and time, taught me valuable lessons about what it means to love God and be church, shaped my thinking about the church and my practice of ministry in the midst of transition, and are present in the pages of this book, not necessarily by name or specific detail, but in spirit. All of them remain in my prayers.

I also want to thank my teaching colleagues and my students in the "Building Skills in Transitional Ministry" course. Their insightful questions and their experiences using the ideas of this book have pushed me to clarify and improve my thinking. Such good students make teaching a joy.

And finally I would like to thank my editor, Beth Ann Gaede. She began by welcoming my rather vague proposal, continued to encourage me through the ups and downs of writing, offered tactful criticism throughout, and has rejoiced with me at the completion.

Which Is Church That?

"What church do you go to?" We go to St. John's. *"Which one is that?"*

- It's the one downtown, at First and Main.
- It's the little white one, out by the lake.
- It's brand new—we still worship in a school.
- It was the first church built in this area.
- It's the one that had all that trouble last year with the minister.
- It's the Presbyterian church.
- It's the Estonian Baptist church.
- It's the biggest congregation in town.
- It's a small church, but very friendly.
- It's the one that welcomes gays and lesbians.
- It's the one that runs the soup kitchen.
- It's the one that has the big Christmas display every year.

- It's the one where all the students go.
- It's the big stone church with a bell tower.
- It's the most progressive church in town.
- It's the one with the biggest Sunday school in town.

Identifying a Church

When I ask people what church they go to and to tell to me in one phrase what distinguishes their church from others, I get a wide range of answers, similar to the descriptions above. People mention location, history, denomination, size, architecture, cultural stance, ethos, program, public presence, internal and external demographics, and theological stance. These are just a few of the ways we commonly identify our churches.

Each of these ways of identifying a church contains a wealth of important information about a congregation. The congregation located "at First and Main" in the decaying old downtown will be very different from the one "out by the lake" in the new condo development beside the golf course. The newest church and the oldest church and the one that "had all that trouble last year" will each be marked by their distinctive history. Congregational size influences a wide range of other factors, especially the dynamics of power and leadership.

Many books have been written about all these ways of describing churches. Church people know that every congregation is different, and the differences have important consequences. A program or strategy that works well in a small church may not work at all in a large church. A church that has been traumatized by a major conflict needs to enter a time of special pastoral care for the whole congregation, rather than just getting on with the usual programs. A church that has a large number of recent immigrant members from one ethnic group will have a very different relationship to the surrounding culture than a church that is mostly composed of people who belong to the majority culture.

Size or history or internal demographics each provide us with a lens through which we can look at a congregation. Each lens helps us to focus clearly on part of the congregation's reality. The resulting analysis can be compared to similar profiles in other congregations, so we can get a sense of what is likely to happen next and what programs and strategies might be effective. Each lens gives us a set of questions to ask and a number of useful hypotheses to try out. The different lenses help us to understand our congregation, so we can better evaluate programs and plan new strategies for mission.

Through each of these lenses, however, we see only one aspect of that complex thing we call congregational identity. I am reminded of the old story of the three blind men who are presented with an elephant and asked to describe it. One man, feeling the trunk, says "An elephant is a kind of snake." The second man, feeling a leg, says, "No, an elephant is a kind of tree." The third blind man, feeling the tail, says, "You are both wrong; an elephant is a kind of broom." When we look at a congregation through a single lens, we see only a partial view of what we are trying to describe and understand, and we may misunderstand completely. No single lens is going to give us a complete picture.

We would have to use all the available lenses to get a comprehensive picture of a congregation. Our imaginary St. John's Church could be assessed in terms of size, demographics, power structure, history, significant individuals, theological stance, denominational policy and polity, and many more lenses. We could add all the resulting views together, creating a detailed description of St. John's. Sociologists call this process "thick description"— the layer upon layer and strand around strand of information needed to fully describe a complex social organism like a congregation. In the end, we would have a huge volume of information—probably many volumes—containing the history, finances, governance, the individual stories as they affected St. John's, and many more topics. All of these studies together would capture the identity of St. John's, in theory at least. However, there are major problems with trying to do a thick description of a congregation. It is too big a project for the vast majority of congregations, and if they did do it, the resulting volume of information would be too big to be used by more than a few people.

Instead of producing the enormous volume of information such an exhaustive description requires, churches generally describe themselves using a few common lenses. For example, when congregations are looking for a new pastor, they usually write a profile of their church, which includes a mission statement, a brief history, a description of activities and programs, the number of members, and a financial statement. Clergy who apply for ministry positions soon learn that these descriptions do not reveal very much. They read between the lines, apply large grains of salt, and phone friends and colleagues in nearby churches to ask, "But what's St. John's *really* like?"

Identity Matters

When we ask, "What is St. John's *really* like?" we are asking the kind of question we often ask about an individual. "I know Dan is an engineer, 45 years old, a father, an avid Lakers fan—but what's he *really* like?" Our question assumes that a congregation, like an individual, has an identity, a uniqueness. Whatever St. John's is like, it is different from all other churches. The lenses help us understand St. John's based on similarities with other churches, and it is certainly useful to consider St. John's as a family-sized church, or a Lutheran church, for example. But our descriptions will tell only a small part of the story. We know there is more to St. John's than being family-sized and Lutheran. No doubt all family-sized Lutheran congregations share many similarities and can learn much from each other, and yet they are all different. The people from St. John's would never say St. John's is just like St Olav's or Augustana. Talk to former clergy from St. John's and tell them stories about what's going on there these days, and they will laugh and say, "That's St. John's, all right. They were always like that!" People who know St. John's know it as a particular church, unique, different from all others.

We are talking about the deepest and most basic kind of identity, but I have to confess right off that I do not know how to define congregational identity, except in some circular way. *Identity is what makes a congregation unique, distinct from all others.* I know of no formula or particular set of criteria that can adequately define identity. In theory, you could add up all the partial descriptions gained from all the lenses above (and any others anyone has thought of) and say that the sum is the identity of the congregation.

But I am not sure the congregation would recognize it as such, and it is obviously necessary that the group being identified recognize itself in the proposed identity statement. For me, the closest analogy to congregational identity is personal identity: what makes you *you* and what makes me *me* is like what makes our imaginary St. John's *St. John's* and not some other church. This is the most basic and profound meaning of identity.

But does identity in this very basic sense matter? Granted that congregations have an identity, why do we need to know it so thoroughly? Isn't the usual handful of studies enough for the purposes of finding a new minister or planning next year's programs? After all, congregational profiles consisting of a few brief descriptions are the time-honored way most denominations describe churches. In my opinion, this type of profile is probably adequate in stable times, when change is happening incrementally and fundamental issues of identity are not challenged. But few mainline churches can count on such stability these days. Many of our congregations seem fated to go through wrenching changes like mergers, closures, redevelopments, and re-missioning processes that cause severe stress and distress at the deepest levels of congregational identity.

At least, this is my experience. I have been an ordained minister in the United Church of Canada for nearly 30 years, the majority of that time working with congregations in transition. In my early years as a pastoral minister, I thought that the major transitions I was seeing in congregations were unusual. I was assuming an old model of church life in which long periods of stability might be interrupted by crises. The church might burn down, or the pastor die suddenly, or something else in the nature of a cataclysmic accident might happen. A church that had more than a couple of such crises over the generations was seen as unfortunate or bad in some way. I certainly assumed this model when I did transitional ministry in the 1980s. My job as an interim minister was to help the congregation heal from the trauma, work through the change, and return to a new stable plateau.

But in twenty-first century North America, few mainline congregations experience long periods of stability. Cataclysmic accidents of one sort and another still occur, but even more important are major social changes such as rural depopulation, the decline of manufacturing industries, and the move of women into the workforce, all of which lead to confusing and stressful changes in congregational life. Perhaps because of social changes, relationships between clergy and congregations and within congregations seem difficult to manage. Serious conflicts, clergy misconduct, and vicious congregational dynamics seem to be more common than they were in the past. If we think of a continuum of change, from renewal (least change) through revitalization to redevelopment (most change), we could say that, in the past, most congregations would need to undertake renewal perhaps once in a decade. Now, congregations are facing the need to revitalize and even redevelop almost that often, and the need for renewal is even more frequent. The new model of transitional ministry is not to get through the change and return to stability, but to get through this change and help the congregation learn the skills to live gracefully in a time of constant change.

The most important skill for change is self-knowledge: that is as true for a congregation as it is for an individual. Congregational leaders now work at increasing the number

of lenses they use to look at their church and are especially interested in tools that will help focus on foundational identity. The search for a comprehensive statement
of identity that the whole congregation can understand and
buy into continues because a congregation that knows its
identity, like a person who knows himself or herself, can
be flexible, open to considering change, and open to respond-
ing to the promptings of the Holy Spirit with new initiatives.

The difficulties remain. How can we sort through the
piles of information we gather in order to arrive at a profile that all can understand and use? A great pile of studies
does not easily translate into a common vision. However,
we understand that when we agree on who we really are,
we will make better decisions about what to do. Clergy and
lay leaders who know their congregation's deep identity
are able to help the people let go of false identity and face
their reality with courage. A clear and clearly articulated
sense of identity does not prevent change as one might
think. A strong sense of identity empowers the congregation to change. They are liberated by the sense of knowing
who they are as they move into the future.

About This Book

This book is about another way of approaching the question of congregational identity, one I believe is more accessible and more immediately useful to congregations.
Instead of piling study upon study, I advocate using an approach I call the personal identity exercise. The personal
identity exercise uses the congregation's knowledge of itself to construct a metaphor, a dynamic model of the congregation as a person. This metaphor is then used to

generate options, priorities, and strategies for future action. Of course, all the lenses—or at least some of them—are still necessary, but this more intuitive and imaginative approach is highly accurate and immediately useful (and lots of fun, too!). I have found that using the personal identity exercise will help congregations and their leaders come to a realistic sense of their identity and to build a new vision and new strategies based on who they really are.

We begin in chapter 1 with a case study that explores the importance of identity and the paralyzing effect of false identity in the life of a congregation. Chapter 2 is an extended biblical and theological reflection on 1 Corinthians 12, particularly on Paul's identification of the congregation in Corinth as a body, and not just any body, but the body of Christ. In Chapter 3, another case study demonstrates how a congregation develops a metaphor of itself as a person and how the implications of the image begin to become evident. Chapter 4 explores the personal identity exercise from a more analytic point of view and gives some guidance on how to prepare for it and conduct it effectively. Chapter 5 looks in detail at how the identity the congregation has articulated in a personal image can be used to locate problem areas, gain a realistic sense of mission possibilities, and plan future action. An epilogue reflects on the possibilities and limitations of the personal identity exercise and concludes with a final story.

This book is full of stories, and all of them are true! At least, they are true to my experience. I know that the wonderful congregations I have worked with over the years will recognize themselves in many of the details if their members happen to read this book. However, the names have been changed and details rearranged and combined in order to make the stories clearer and more effective for my purposes. The one story that does not come from my own experience is the "Rosebud Report" at the end of chapter 4, which is included as an example of excellent reporting by a congregation.

The stories are included for more than illustration. The personal identity exercise encourages the congregation to tell itself stories about the person it chooses as an image. Narrative teaches us in open and inviting ways because stories do not need experts to understand or interpret them. The stories in this book are meant to be used as a part of the personal identity exercise, giving examples of how actual churches have articulated and used a personal identity image. In my experience, when a congregation hears a story about another church (especially if it is in quite a different situation), the story sparks members' imagination to think about *their* story and exactly how it is different. The stories in this book tell all I know, and more, about congregational identity. I pray they will enlarge the understanding of readers and engage many more congregations in the work of articulating a realistic and usable identity.

Hilltop Church and Hillside Church are two

congregations of the same denomination just two miles apart in similar suburban communities. The two churches, which were both built in the 1950s, have been declining for 20 years. Years ago, as finances became a problem, the judicatory urged them to merge the two congregations to make one effective church with one minister, one building, and one mission to the surrounding community. Some of the key lay leaders were enthusiastic, and the amalgamation took place. But it never got beyond the shared-minister stage. The finances were never put together, none of the property was sold, and the two churches did no more together than they had always done. Ten years later, when Rev. Howard was appointed as the interim minister, it was clear that the two congregations were suspicious of each other and had a poor working relationship.

The first decision the two congregations made was to end the merger. Although the separation left two tiny groups with severely limited human and financial resources and a very unclear future, each congregation experienced an immediate feeling of relief and a sudden burst of energy. In reflecting with the leaders of the congregations, Rev. Howard suggested that their merger was as if some well-intentioned person had seen old Mrs. Jones at one end of the street, lonely and struggling to keep her house and garden in good order, and old Mr. Smith at the other end of the street in the same sort of situation, and thought, "The solution is obvious: these two people should get married, and all their problems will be solved!" The congregational leaders were delighted with this absurd analogy and were even able to admit a certain affection for each other—as long as they didn't have to get married!

^ACase_{of} Mistaken Identity

We begin our exploration of congregational identity with a case study of a congregation that has become confused about who it is. St. Paul's is not an actual church, but a composite of many churches I, and probably you, have known. It is typical of the thousands of churches that mainline Protestant denominations built in the years following the Second World War and that flourished throughout the 1950s and '60s but that are now struggling. Sometimes they are called "one generation churches," for many of them have already closed. Much of the angst in the mainline is centered around these churches, and they deserve a close look.

Churches of any sort can lose their identity. At the end of the chapter we take a brief look at another church, First Church Birrville, a large, well-established congregation. First Church was built generations before the Second World War, yet it too suffers from a loss of identity.

Starting Out at St. Paul's Church

When the Rev. Sue Alexander began her interim ministry appointment at St. Paul's, she didn't know much about the congregation. The judicatory officials knew that St. Paul's needed an interim—a long history of decline, a series of short and unhappy calls, reports of conflict and bad behavior, and now a looming financial crisis all indicated deep problems. However, the members of St. Paul's were angry at not being allowed to call a "real minister." They figured that they had already had a number of short-term ministers, including an interim minister, and they didn't think another one would do them any good. Many in the congregation feared that the interim was just a way to close them down. Sue knew it was not going to be an easy assignment.

Looking out at the congregation on her first Sunday, Sue's heart faltered. The two older women who made up the choir were really pleased and said that everyone had come to check out the new minister. What Sue saw scattered around the sanctuary was about 25 adults and three young children. A dozen of the adults were older women in their seventies or eighties and there was one man in the same age group. One man and half a dozen women were younger seniors in the 65 to 75 age group. A handful of women looked to be in their fifties or sixties, and one younger woman sat by herself at the back. The children seemed to be attached to one of the younger seniors— their grandmother, Sue guessed.

The sanctuary was gloomy and shabby; even the banners on the walls looked dirty. The elderly woman who played the organ did her best, but the music was muffled and uncertain, and Sue couldn't tell if anyone besides herself was singing. Sue had carefully prepared for her first service, focusing on affirmations of the past ministry of St. Paul's and hope for the future, but the response from the congregation was muted, even sullen. The word that kept running through her mind was "dispirited." St. Paul's seemed to have lost its spirit, its vital force. She felt her own spirits sink as she struggled to inject some life into the worship. She wondered what she had gotten herself into. She began to suspect that what the congregation feared was true—that St. Paul's was likely to close soon.

At her first meeting with the St. Paul's board, Sue took stock of the leadership team—six elderly women and the elderly man she had met on Sunday and a retired man who announced that he no longer attended worship. Three other board members were missing, but Sue was told they no longer attended the meetings because of health problems. Sue was asked to open the meeting with prayer, and she had never prayed more fervently for the presence and guidance of the Holy Sprit. The meeting was long, tedious, and cantankerous, with only two of the women and the retired man who didn't come to church dominating the agenda. Sue sat there in frustration wondering what she should say when they finally reached the minister's report, the last item on the list. She decided to ask them a question: "What kind of church is St. Paul's? What's special about it?"

At first there was silence as they contemplated this strange question. Finally Beth, one of the elderly women, said firmly, "We are a family church, a real neighborhood church." And all agreed. "But there are only three kids in the Sunday school," Fred said. Beth responded fiercely, "We just need to get a young minister with a family to get the

Sunday school going again and bring in the young people!"
It seemed that this conversation had taken place many
times before, as all the others both nodded in agreement
and bowed their heads in sorrow. Sue was wise enough to
know that she had just heard an expression from the heart
of this sad little church.

> We are a family church.
> We are a real neighborhood church.
> We just need to get a young minister with a family.

"We are a family church . . ."

Beth had married Jim just before he went overseas in 1940,
and their first child was born in early 1941. Three more
children were born in quick succession after Jim returned
in 1945. Fred was a veteran as well. He married an English
girl, Helen, and brought her back home after the war; they
had three children born almost the same dates as Beth's
three youngest. Along with hundreds of couples just like
them, Beth and Jim and Fred and Helen took advantage of
special mortgage rates for veterans and bought a small
bungalow in one of the new suburbs at the edge of the city,
where they settled down to raise their families.

By the late 1940s, these young parents began to feel
the need for a church in their neighborhood, especially for
their children's Christian education. The denomination was
by this time quite familiar with the process of establishing
new churches and quickly appointed a retired minister to
canvass the neighborhood and set up the congregation.
St. Paul's was born. For the first couple of years, the rapidly growing congregation met in a school, but by 1950 the

sanctuary was built. Almost immediately, as the flood of children kept coming, a Christian education wing was added.

St Paul's flourished. The Sunday school was huge; everyone said there were 550 children, but that was probably an exaggeration. Weekdays and Saturdays were busy with church and community-based programs and sports leagues for every age group of both girls and boys. Adults had a women's group for every morning of the week, and men's groups on Saturdays. The choir and the couples' club were popular and special events like bazaars and teas and potluck suppers involved everyone. The board and most of the committees were staffed by the men, who also looked after the building and the grounds.

As Sue listened to the stories about those wonderful early years at St. Paul's, she began to understand what being "a family church" meant. Of course, it meant lots of young couples with lots of young children, but she could see that, for the St. Paul's congregation, a family church was more than just a church with families: it was a church fully oriented to the needs of young parents and children. Raising a good family was the supreme goal in life for all these people it seemed, and the role of the church was to support and enhance that work. In those early years, very little happened at St. Paul's that wasn't focused on the well-being of the congregation's families. When Sue understood this total devotion to family, it helped her understand the enormity of the loss when the children left.

The children left in the '60s, first a few and then almost all of them. The present members of St. Paul's sometimes spoke as if a pied piper had spirited all the children away, but actually, nothing unusual happened. St. Paul's simply experienced the cultural changes that happened to everyone in the '60s. Television and teen culture made church seem boring; sports and other children's activities were available on Sundays and offered an attractive alternative. St. Paul's leaders were a little slow to realize that the average age of the congregation's children was increasing and that youth groups now required more of their energy and attention than did Sunday school. The result was that far fewer teenagers were involved in youth groups in the '60s than there had been children in the '50s. Beth's oldest daughter stayed in the youth group until she left for college, but her three younger brothers all quit before they were 15. One of Fred's daughters went to the youth group for a few years, but the other daughter and his son refused to go.

In the '70s, St. Paul's finally began to work seriously at engaging the remaining teenagers with more sophisticated programs and better trained leaders, but their efforts didn't seem to help. As the baby boom began to fade, the trend accelerated: fewer young children began Sunday school and more teens left. The ones who did remain in the teen groups left as soon as they graduated from high school. They went away to college, or to work, or to start their own families, and they didn't come back to St. Paul's.

At first the exodus was hardly noticed. The children did not attend the worship service in the sanctuary in those days (they were in classes held in the Sunday school hall), and the number of adults in worship remained fairly constant. Then the adults began to leave, too. For some parents, once their children "graduated" from Sunday school, there didn't seem much point in going to church. Some adults moved to other parts of the city or even other cities. For many more, the cultural changes in family life made church seem not a necessary and fundamental part of life, but one option among others. Women entered the workforce in great numbers and were not at home during the day to attend a women's group or bake brownies for the spring tea. Busy parents' evenings and weekends were filled with household chores and shopping and family time. Many families had increased leisure time and disposable income, and the availability of Sunday shopping and recreational activities meant that there were many other things to do on a Sunday morning. The family car made all these enticing possibilities accessible. As the '80s began, St. Paul's could hardly avoid noticing that not just the children but many of the adults had disappeared.

The two elderly ladies who made up the choir now showed Sue the careful records they had kept of attendance at weekly worship and Sunday school. Sue could see that attendance since 1960 had halved every decade. In 1960, average attendance was about 400—250 adults and 150 children and youth. Ten years later, it was about 200—175 adults and 25 children and youth. In 1980, it was about 100—90 adults and 10 children and youth. That was when it was no longer possible to deny that there was serious decline and real concern began to be expressed by the leadership.

In the early '90s, most of the members said that the children—theirs or others like them—would be back when they settled down, married, and had their own children. They would feel the same call their parents did to include church in their family life. But that didn't happen at St. Paul's or at many other churches. Except in a few places, the baby boomers left church in their teens and never looked back. Of the seven children in Beth's and Fred's families, only Beth's oldest daughter was active in church where she lived.

Besides, families were not like they used to be, and Fred and Beth were deeply confused and saddened at what their children were doing—there were several divorces among them, a common-law relationship, and two marriages to people from different ethnic backgrounds. And none of their grandchildren were baptized or active in church.

Sue contemplated this story of loss and could see why the congregation seemed so depressed. The claim "We are a family church" was a tattered flag; not only had their particular families grown up and gone, but there were no young families at all. Beth and Fred were typical of the congregation now, and they didn't even think of themselves as families, now that they were widowed and their children and grandchildren were scattered all around the country.

Beth clung to the old flag and Fred rejected it, but they were equally grief-stricken and equally confused about what to do.

"We are a real neighborhood church . . ."

Before the war, the area where St. Paul's would be was mostly rough bush and farmland. On the road leading to the city were a few small stores and businesses. During the war, a couple of manufacturing plants opened up along this road, a few houses were built, and the business area began to grow.

When the veterans came home, they did not go back to the farms and small towns where they had lived before. They came to the cities, which expanded rapidly. The regional authority took over land for new subdivisions and installed basic services and roads. Developers built the houses, and veterans like Jim and Fred moved in, thanks to special mortgage programs. In the space of 10 years, what had been unimproved land became a suburban neighborhood—this one called Meadow Park. The neighborhood included stores and schools, professional services such as doctors and dentists, a recreation center, a cinema, and churches. St. Paul's was the first church built in the area, but by the end of the 1950s there were many more.

As Sue walked around Meadow Park, she asked herself, what did the word *neighborhood* mean for Jim and Beth and Fred and Helen, and the thousands like them, in the late 1940s? As she talked to the older residents, Sue could see that *neighborhood* meant something more than just an area on a map. It meant a community of people living together in a self-sufficient village built on the values of family, stability, and security. Photos of Meadow Park in the '50s showed rows of small bungalows all alike, row after row, with no trees. But in the hearts of the veterans, it looked like a small town of the 1920s, the kind of place where families had lived for generations and everybody knew everybody else.

This modest vision was a longed-for paradise for people who were raised in the depression and came to adulthood in World War II. Sue heard the stories about how the depression had fragmented many families, especially in small towns and rural areas: men suffered the shame of not being able to provide for their families and left to find work; children were sent to relatives better able to care for them; young people had to quit school and get what work they could to help the family. The war rescued many from poverty, but at the price of terror, trauma, and more social dislocation. The men, and some of the women, went to war, while those who stayed home carried on as best they could, or moved to the cities to work in war industries. Couples and sweethearts were separated, young men and women were wounded in body, mind, and spirit, and plans for careers and families were put on hold for years. Not everyone had only bad experiences: many men enjoyed life in the services and learned skills and trades, and many women got to leave home and earn their own living away from the social conformity of rural and small town life.

The returning veterans did not go back to the farms and small towns they had left because the jobs were now in the cities, yet they wanted to live by small-town family values. They viewed suburbs like Meadow Park as their new hometown where they would know everyone and their families. They expected that the little houses they bought would be their homes forever and their children would grow up to live nearby. Churches were at the heart of this vision; it seemed that every suburb had to have a church of each denomination within walking distance. A church of St. Paul's denomination already had been built only two miles from Meadow Park, but that was someone else's neighborhood; Meadow Park people had to have their own church. They were not interested in having a big church; they wanted one just big enough for the neighborhood.

In the minds of the original members, St. Paul's was the church of Meadow Park, Sue realized, as a village church was once the church of that particular village. The founding members of the congregation all remembered the time when St. Paul's was the only church in Meadow Park, and all the mainline Protestant denominations worshiped there. Although that was for a very brief time—about one year—it seemed central to the story. Fred told Sue that the decline at St. Paul's began when the other churches were built. That was clearly not true, according to the statistical record, but it was the first of many changes that threatened the identity of St. Paul's as *the* neighborhood church.

As the largest church and the founding church of its neighborhood, St. Paul's was a prominent member of the community. Anything to do with children and families was of particular interest to St. Paul's, and you could find St. Paul's people on the school board, the recreation center board, and the district planning committee, as well as leading scouting and sports programs for boys and girls. While St. Paul's was progressive in its social and theological positions, members kept a watchful eye on local businesses: parents like Beth and Jim were clear that stores would not get away with under-the-counter sales of cigarettes (or worse) to minors. The values of the neighborhood were solidly represented and promoted by St. Paul's people.

One of the other high values of the community was caring for neighbors. Anyone in the neighborhood who had trouble—sickness, unemployment, a death in the family—could count on the immediate generosity of St. Paul's. Sue heard stories about the year of the flood when several houses down by the river were badly damaged, and St. Paul's became the relief center where people were helped and goods donated. The year St. Nicholas Church burned down, St. Paul's welcomed that congregation and shared the building with them. St. Paul's was the first congregation in Meadow Park to have an AA group meeting in its building, a move that was considered daring at the time.

They also extended their generosity to the wider world; the denomination's mission fund was well supported, as were local charities.

As the social and cultural changes of the '60s began, Meadow Park began to change, too. In the late '50s, as women began to join the workforce in large numbers, the women of St. Paul's responded in a creative and progressive manner. They opened a preschool and daycare in the church basement. St. Paul's Daycare was a service to the community and was open to everyone, regardless of church affiliation. The church would provide safe and stimulating care for young children and support younger families. The daycare was a proud part of the St. Paul's identity as both a family and a neighborhood church.

The need for daycare in Meadow Park was not just about changing family patterns; it was part of changes in the neighborhood and in the very concept of neighborhood. Quite a few of Beth and Jim's friends moved away in the '60s. Men did not stay with one company forever, and work took them elsewhere, or they prospered and bought bigger homes in newer suburbs. Other people moved in, and these new people often did not see themselves as joining a community of neighbors but as simply moving to a "nice neighborhood"—a place with tree-lined streets and good schools, convenient to the city. The new people didn't seem to find much of a place for church in their lives. One of the denomination's churches was closed and the congregation merged with St. Paul's. Although St. Paul's was only a mile away from the church that closed, most of the members never actually made the transition. St. Paul's did benefit from the proceeds of the sale of the building. The concept of Meadow Park as a village where you would settle down for generations was replaced by Meadow Park as a suburb of a big city. "Neighborhood" had less to do with community and more to do with an area on the map.

Changes to the Meadow Park area accelerated through the '70s and '80s. The business district became rundown as the malls and later big-box stores proved more appealing. The modest post-war bungalows that lined the streets seemed cramped and shabby by contemporary standards, but the value of the land rose dramatically. Many of Jim and Beth's friends, with their children now grown up and gone, sold their houses for what seemed like fabulous sums and moved to condos in the suburbs. Asian immigrants snapped up the old houses and tore them down to build much larger ones. Sue looked at the census reports and was amazed at how quickly and massively change had come. Meadow Park was now part of a multicultural urban center. One of the remaining churches of St. Paul's denomination was sold and became a Sikh temple. The elementary school after years of declining enrollment was full again, and the principal reported that the children came from dozens of different language groups. The business district was bustling with many interesting shops and ethnic restaurants.

By the year 2000, Meadow Park had disappeared as a distinct area, and only the old-timers even remembered the name. It was now just part of an urban area, with urban values and culture. St. Paul's, the village church of the Meadow Park community, had lost its anchor, its point of reference.

"We just need a young minister with a family . . ."

Every time Sue heard the phrase, "We just need a young minister with a family," she had to grit her teeth and take a deep breath: she was clearly not a young (male was assumed) minister with young children. She was middle-aged, divorced, and the mother of two grown children who did not even live in the same city. It was hard not to feel criticized just for being who she was.

The odd thing was, when she looked at the "rogues gallery" in the narthex, she could see from the pictures of her predecessors that St. Paul's had never had that wonderful being, a young minister with a family. Their founding minister was a retired man pressed back into service due to the shortage of clergy following the war. The three ministers from 1950 to 1970 all looked like fatherly types—they would have been much older than the average age of the adults in the congregation. In 1971, St. Paul's called a man who would have been a contemporary of the founding members of the congregation. He stayed for nearly 14 years and retired from St. Paul's in 1985; he did have a daughter, but no one remembered her too clearly. From 1985 to 1995 there were four ministers, who stayed two or three years each. Two of the four were women, and all were clearly middle-aged and older. Then there was a man who stayed five years and retired, and then came Sue. No young minister with a family.

She wondered if there had been some much-loved youth leader in the past, or a candidate for ministry who had captured the affection and imagination of the congregation, but no, Beth and Fred couldn't remember anyone of that sort. Starting in the 1980s there had always been a paid Sunday school coordinator, usually a university student, and always a woman; they came and went and none of them seemed to leave much of an impression. For a while, in the '60s and early '70s, there was a youth leader, but most of the youth work was done by a younger couple from the congregation.

Sue probed gently to find where the idea came from that a young minister with a family would bring back the children and young people. It just seemed to be something that "everyone knew." The need to call a young minister with a family actually seemed to function as a comment about the past more than about the future; the minister who had the 14-year pastorate from 1971 to 1985 was widely seen as responsible for the disappearance of all the young people, although the exodus had begun well before his term.

From what Fred and Beth remembered, it was about 1980 when the leaders of St. Paul's began to realize they were sliding into serious trouble. The ranks of the founding generation were thinning out, and they were not being replaced. The whole boomer generation was missing, and the few younger couples who came seemed unwilling to do their share of all the work it takes to keep a church running smoothly (not to mention the money that is required). However, most of the congregation did not yet see a crisis: there was still enough money (although the finance committee was balancing the budget by spending endowments), many of the old familiar friends were still there, and the worship, social life, and pastoral care continued to be meaningful for them.

Beth, who for years had been the unpaid coordinator of St. Paul's Daycare, withdrew after Jim died suddenly of a heart attack in 1981, and it seemed there was no one who wanted to take over such a big volunteer job. One of the paid daycare staff offered to take it over as a private business and pay rent to the church, and the offer was eagerly accepted. The daycare continued—and continues—to operate, and the St. Paul's people still refer to it with pride as a program of the church, but in fact, neither the staff nor the children and their families have any other contact with St. Paul's. The revenue from the daycare now makes up over 30 percent of the church's annual budget.

In 1985, when the minister retired, the whole congregation woke as from a long sleep and realized that St. Paul's was not what it used to be. This was the time when everyone began to say, "We need a young minister with a family," someone who would appeal to the younger generation, and whose children (and wife, of course—although you weren't supposed to say that) would draw other similar families into the church through their connections in the school and the neighborhood. The judicatory had other ideas: after a long pastorate and with the congregation in serious decline, an interim minister should come and help them plan for their future. The congregation reluctantly agreed and spent two years solemnly considering new visions for the future, but they were not really committed to doing anything new. Nothing changed; the exodus continued.

As the founding generation retired, many more members of that cohort left, some to other neighborhoods and some to the busy lives of active seniors. The older ones also began to experience health problems and a decline in energy; Fred's wife Helen got cancer and was sick for years before she died, and everyone agreed that Fred had never been the same since. Life at St. Paul's was simplified: projects and programs came to an end as the leaders left or resigned; groups that continued met in someone's house; board meetings were held in the daytime because people didn't like going out at night. The building was still busy since St. Paul's now rented space to a Chinese congregation of another denomination and to numerous community groups. The congregation still tended to talk about these rentals as a community ministry, but there was little contact with these groups and organizations except for the monthly check and some tension around the use of the kitchen and the state of the washrooms.

St. Paul's leaders were getting tired and thought it should be someone else's turn to take over, but there was no one else, so the faithful old guard carried on. The building began to be neglected; there were so few men anymore, and they weren't supposed to get up on ladders. Worship was depressing, with fewer and fewer people scattered around the sanctuary; visitors who walked in the door once almost never came back. Board meetings were difficult, with a couple of members dominating every discussion; the others made any excuse not to go, and two or three people often made all the decisions.

The last few ministers since the interim minister tried without success to persuade the congregation to engage in the work the interim minister had suggested to them, or at least to think about where they were going and what they should do. However, the congregation seemed to have no will or energy for this work. By the time Sue arrived, St. Paul's was a very unhealthy congregation: unhappy, angry, stuck, and frightened—totally focused on survival. Even they couldn't really believe that a young minister with a family would save them—they just couldn't think of anything else.

A Church Stuck in the Past

Sue met with Carol, one of the regional judicatory staff, to share what she had learned about St. Paul's in her first six months. She mentioned how she had found such profound—and troubling—meaning in Beth's observation at the first board meeting in September.

We are a family church.
We are a real neighborhood church.
We just need to get a young minister with a family.

Carol laughed at this self-description. "Lord, they sure are stuck in the past!" That much was certainly clear, Sue agreed. Poor St. Paul's! Not only their own families, but the very concept of family had changed; not only their own neighborhood, but the very concept of neighborhood had changed; and as for a young minister with a family rescuing them, why would a young man want to come to such a depressing place? Anyway, most seminarians now were middle-aged women. St. Paul's was stuck in the 1950s and couldn't function in the twenty-first century.

But why? After all, some post-war churches had not only survived, but thrived; what were *they* doing that was different? Carol mentally reviewed the list of these congregations, and couldn't think of any particular factor. Throughout the region, all of the post-war congregations had experienced a crisis between 1970 and 1980 as the baby boom ended, and half of them had merged with other congregations or limped along a few years and then closed. Of the churches that had survived into the 90s, about a third were in serious trouble (like St. Paul's), a third were struggling, and a third were doing reasonably well. A huge range of factors were involved in the outcome—clergy and lay leadership, community demographics, location and architecture of the building, financial security, and mission and programs. Everything the church experts say is true, Carol concluded; there are many factors that contribute to the health of a congregation, and you could not just point to one thing.

Nor could you point to one thing to explain a failure to thrive. In some ways, you could see St. Paul's as the victim of a perfect storm—not a huge violent storm, Carol and Sue decided, but a sort of "dust storm" of small events and factors that gradually eroded the substance of the congregation. They had not had particularly strong clergy leaders, and several key lay leaders had died, moved, or withdrawn at critical points. They lost the boomer generation (so had almost all the other congregations), and almost all their new neighbors were from other faith groups and not likely to join any Christian church. The building was set in the heart of Meadow Park, in the midst of a tangle of small residential streets where no one would see it; it was poorly maintained, looked shabby and uninviting, and lacked accessible washrooms and nursery facilities. St. Paul's had gained some financial security due to a merger in the early '70s and substantial rental income since then, but that security allowed them to ignore the demographic crisis too long. Its mission and programs were all about young families and children: when those disappeared, there was little energy and purpose left. St. Paul's might have overcome one or two of these factors and gone on to thrive, but all together, they made the present state seem inevitable.

Carol was sympathetic; it looked like Sue was going to have to lead St. Paul's into a merger or a straightforward closure, never an easy or pleasant task. Actually, Sue said, many members of the congregation were coming to the same conclusion as they remembered their history and finally faced up to the full extent of their decline. Some of the leaders were beginning to feel relieved as they imagined a time when they would no longer have to worry about their church. But of course there were others, the ones who would rather die than lose St. Paul's. And then there were some who still thought St. Paul's could have a future—and not just because they would find the "magic minister" who would re-create the past!

The odd thing was, Sue reflected, St. Paul's was stuck in the '50s, but its people were not. Their lives had changed a great deal since the '50s, but they had gone on living. Fred was not trying to pretend he was 30 years old, and Beth wasn't dreaming of looking after babies again! As individuals, they were not stuck in nostalgia: they were by and large enjoying their lives as seniors and were coping with the inevitable losses and deficits with courage and humor. In fact, they were quite critical of other seniors they knew who were not being realistic about their age, or who were making life difficult for others by refusing to make necessary decisions. What was it about their church that made it impossible to live in the present with the same courage and openness? Just saying they were stuck in the past wasn't a very useful analysis of their situation.

A False Identity

The more Sue thought about it, the more it seemed to her that St. Paul's was behaving like a person out of touch with his or her actual situation. It was rather like what Fred would be doing if he were absolutely refusing to acknowledge his age—she was diverted by the thought of Fred (in reality, a wise and mature gentleman) trying to pretend he was a young parent again or had a career to make at the plant. Or imagine Beth wasting her time longing to have more children instead of enjoying her grandchildren and her freedom as a senior, as she did in reality. St. Paul's was pretending to be something it no longer was. That was understandable—the '50s and '60s had been such good times for the church—and Sue could see why the St. Paul's people were tempted to dwell on that time. They were behaving like the high school football hero who is still telling the stories of the Great Game and showing off his trophies 50 years later—sad and a bit ridiculous.

But living in a false identity is worse than pathetic, Sue reflected: it is disabling. When we are mistaken about who we are, nothing works. Holding on to a false identity is worse than merely being confused about your identity. A false identity creates a false certainty about what you do, and yet apparently rational choices never seem to work out. As Sue knew from psychology courses as well as from her pastoral experience, a person's sense of identity is so important that a threat to one's identity is often perceived as a threat to life itself and is accordingly resisted with ferocious determination—even when the identity is false. Perhaps denial and resistance is especially strong when the identity is false, she reflected. People trying to live a life that isn't really theirs seem desperate, as if they must fight extra hard to maintain this identity in the face of assaults from reality.

This idea of a false identity at St. Paul's made sense out of a whole lot of things, Sue thought. She remembered that first board meeting and the painful exchange between Beth and Fred, when Beth said, "We are a family church, a real neighborhood church." Fred had responded, "But there are only three kids in the Sunday school." And Beth insisted fiercely, "We just need to get a young minister with a family to get the Sunday school going again and bring in the young people!" You could see the whole dilemma in that exchange: St. Paul's was clearly not a family and neighborhood church anymore, and everyone knew that; everyone knew there were only three children in the Sunday school and all the other sad facts of decline. But no one could afford to admit it, because the threat to the congregation's sense of identity was too painful. Instead, there was the completely unrealistic solution proposed: find the magic young minister who would somehow reaffirm and restore their identity.

The idea of a false identity also helped explain all those failed renewal strategies and programs in the '80s and '90s, including the interim ministry. The judicatory had grown very frustrated with St. Paul's failure to change. The judicatory made sure that St. Paul's had many consultants, and two whole years of interim, but the congregation continued to resist all change. Sue could see now that St. Paul's was clinging to its identity as to life itself and wasn't about to accept any change that would threaten its identity.

The cost of such an unproductive strategy was high. Not only did the decline continue, but the people became more and more angry, depressed, and guilt-ridden. They still saw themselves as a family and neighborhood church, but as a failed one; and someone must be to blame for this failure. They blamed their ministers, the judicatory, each other, and, most of all, themselves. Now their church was dying, and it was all their fault—if only the board hadn't done this, or the judicatory done that; if only the last minister had stayed, or left sooner; if only they could just call a nice young minister with a family. The sadness, guilt, and anger hung over everything like the dust in the narthex. This miasma of depression was what made visitors leave so fast and made even the members more and more reluctant to come (and they felt guilty for that, too). From the members' point of view, they were doing everything in their power and nothing was working. When Sue saw the patterns clearly, she was moved with a deep compassion for the people of St. Paul's.

She was also really excited by this concept of a false identity and how much of St. Paul's situation it explained. She was pretty sure she was right on the mark, and she was eager to check it out with the congregation but thought she might first meet with Beth and Fred. And then she stopped herself. So what if it was all true? What if she could use her brilliant analysis to force Beth and Fred and the others to see what was going on—then what? What would it achieve? She could imagine that admitting St. Paul's was no longer a family neighborhood church would just confirm their worst fears and leave them more depressed than ever. Facing up to the reality of St. Paul's situation would be very painful, and if that's all she had to offer, why would they listen to her? Sue suspected that they would somehow find a way to deny what she said, and her reports would join the big stack of previous efforts to help the congregation understand itself.

Sue thought about the poster that hung on her wall during a bad time in her own life. It showed a raggedy doll with an agonized expression being squeezed through the ringer of an old-fashioned washing machine. The caption said, "The truth will make you free, but first it will make you miserable."[1] Sometimes truth was painful, especially the kind of truth that comes from self-knowledge, but if there was some promise that the pain was going to lead somewhere—to freedom or healing or reconciliation—you could face it. But without that promise? Sue knew that the generation that had grown up in the Depression and come to adulthood in the war had a lot of experience facing painful truths, but there had to be some hope as well.

What kind of hope could she hold out to the people of St. Paul's that might allow them to bear the pain of questioning their identity? She could not honestly promise them a bright and glorious future. They no longer had the human resources to rebuild their congregation, and the financial resources were disappearing fast. They might have to close: St. Paul's might have to die. Sue wondered what the hope for a congregation at the end of its life might be. Was there a gospel, good news for congregations? Could there be resurrection for St. Paul's if it had to die? Sue realized she needed to do a lot more thinking, studying, and praying before the idea of false identity could be offered to the congregation. She needed to study the biblical and theological foundations of the church, the sources of their common hope.

A Case of Lost Identity

As a complement to the story of St. Paul's, we take a brief look at another church that has lost its identity. The common feature of these two stories, and in my experience, the common factor at work in all churches that lose their identity, is demographic change. Readers may find this a useful example to share with a congregation that is beginning to work on its identity.

First Church had stood at the corner of First and Main at the center of Birrville long before there was even a traffic light there. Right across the street was the old Birrville town hall, and the church was always an influential participant in civic issues. In the past, the mayor and many of Birrville's leading citizens were members of First Church, and it was well known that many important issues for the town were debated and resolved at the men's breakfast group or the women's auxiliary meetings. First Church had a tradition of strong, independent-minded preachers, and many former mayors had squirmed in the oak pews as the minister led the congregation to reflect on community values. People said there would not have been a food bank, or an alternate school for troubled kids, or a decent library in town without First Church. In fact, Birrville just wouldn't have been the same without the fine ministry of this church. First Church was at the center of Birrville in more ways than one.

The town of Birrville prospered and grew modestly over the years, but Marbridge, the next town to the west, really boomed in the '80s and '90s. The authorities decided to realign boundaries and put Birrville and a couple of other towns into a new municipality with Marbridge at its center. The people from Birrville fought this measure as long as they could, with First Church leading the campaign, but the planning experts spoke of progress and efficiencies of scale and transportation corridors; the new municipality was formed a few years ago. Now the old Birrville town hall has been turned into condos with trendy shops on the street level.

First Church is still there, where it has always been. Attendance is still good, and generations of faithful stewardship have ensured a healthy financial situation, yet the church seems to be drifting. The members have tried to establish a strong relationship with the new city council in Marbridge, but the new mayor and most of the council

members are not from Birrville and it's hard to get them to
come to events. There is a lot of bitterness at First Church
about how its generations of faithful service to the town
are being ignored, and many members have joined the campaign to get a good candidate from Birrville for mayor at
the next election. A few of the members are saying they
should just forget the glory days of power and influence
and move on. But move on to where? What is First Church,
if it is not at the center of Birrville's life?

2

You Are the Body of Christ

Our fictional St. Paul's Church is in such sad shape that it is tempting to just let it die. According to many reasonable criteria, this congregation is no longer really a church. It has lost all sense of mission, and it is so small and weak that it can no longer fulfill all the functions that the denomination expects of congregations. The members are dispirited and depressed; the congregation is most unattractive and would seem to have no possibility of spiritual or numerical growth. That St. Paul's continues to exist seems to have more to do with social-psychological factors than with Christian faith and practice. The few remaining members are deeply bonded with each other and desperately want their little community to stay the same in a world that is changing all around them. They are good, decent people who want to help each other and to live well in the world, and they certainly need and deserve pastoral care, but does that make them a church?

Sue's fundamental question about her ministry at St. Paul's is: What kind of hope can she hold out to the congregation that might allow them to bear the pain of questioning their false identity and facing their reality? The hope that they have now, that a magic minister will come and restore them to their former state, is a false one and just keeps leading them deeper and deeper into despair. What they need is the kind of hope that is given by the Spirit, a true and realistic hope that can ground them in a foundational identity while they come to grips with their present and face the challenges of their future. In short, St. Paul's needs to hear the Gospel for churches. They need to go back to the foundations of Christian hope in the New Testament.

Articulating the foundations of hope and good news for congregations is our task in this chapter. We will be looking at the church in Corinth through the words of Paul in 1 Corinthians to see how he named their identity. We will reflect on the implications for congregations in the twenty-first century, not just St. Paul's, but all congregations. At the end of the chapter, there is a story about how one church found its ground of hope.

Finding the Foundations of Hope and Identity

Besides looking at the New Testament, we might look for the foundations of hope for congregations in the ecclesiology (the theology of the church) of our denominational tradition. However, even though I am a theologian with a specialty in ecclesiology, I have realized in my pastoral ministry that theology about the church is seldom helpful for congregations. When theologians talk about "the Church," they are usually talking about the Church-in-general, the "one, holy, catholic and apostolic Church,"[1] a rather abstract concept. You and I don't actually see the Church or get to worship and work in it. What we get instead is a particular church. Theologians tend to talk about congregations and local churches as manifestations of the Church. The assumption is that the Church is the ideal church, the one to which all those wonderful descriptions apply—one, holy, universal, and faithful to the apostolic tradition. Most Christians, I think, feel sure that their particular church falls far short of the ideal of the Church.

The Church and what is said about it doesn't seem very relevant to decisions about whether to repair the roof or hire a youth worker, or whether to go to two services on Sunday morning or do something different on Saturday night. In fact, the Church can be a heavy ideal for a local congregation, especially when our North American faith in progress and success gets mixed up with our Christian faith. Leaders of many congregations feel ashamed if their church is not big and getting bigger. "The other, big box church down the road must be a better church than we are, closer to the ideal Church—look how they're growing!" people say. Small churches, churches in conflict, ordinary churches—most churches!—feel inadequate when they compare themselves to the Church.

The New Testament, on the other hand, comes from a time before theology was an organized discipline and speaks to the experience of particular groups of believers. Nowhere is that clearer than in Paul's letters, especially in the letters to the Christians in Corinth. In my experience, a

Bible study of 1 Corinthians is a great place to begin looking for good news for congregations. This letter sets out
so much material for a community to reflect on that any
congregation, in any circumstances, could benefit from
studying it.

The Christian Community in Corinth

Sometime in the middle of the first century, less than 20
years after Jesus's crucifixion and resurrection, Paul wrote
a series of letters to the Christians gathered in Corinth.
These letters were not theological essays, although Paul
worked out a great deal of his theology in them. They were
not gospels, either, although Paul referred here and there
to incidents in the life of Jesus. And they were not Paul's
personal testimonial to his own faith, although he was not
shy about using himself as an example. These letters are
quite simply letters. What is more, they are replies to other
letters and messages that Paul had received, so they deal
with specific issues and situations and questions raised
by the Corinthian Christians. The other side of the story,
the letters from Corinth, are all lost, and we are left with
only Paul's responses. We are like someone finding a bundle
of letters in an old trunk in the attic—with the added difficulty that some of the pages seem to have got mixed up
and some seem to be missing.

Although we have no direct word from the Corinthian
Christians, we do know a lot from historians and arche-
ologists about life in the city of Corinth in the middle of
the first century. A number of features about life in first-
century Corinth make it easy for contemporary Christians
to identify with the Christians there. First, Corinth was a

city with many similarities to modern North American cities. Second, the Christians of Corinth and the surrounding area gathered in a number of small groups, not unlike our congregations. Third, the Corinthian Christians were struggling with what it means to be a Christian community in their place and time, just as we do.

The City of Corinth

The city of Corinth controlled one of the main commercial routes between Italy and Asia, and had prospered for thousands of years. Two hundred years before Paul arrived, in 146 B.C.E., however, Corinth had resisted the advancing Roman Empire and paid the ultimate price: the Roman armies destroyed the city, killed most of the men, and sold the women and children into slavery. Only a few of the wealthiest citizens escaped into exile. For 100 years, the only residents of Corinth were squatters among the ruins. Then in 44 B.C.E., Julius Caesar reestablished the city as a Roman colony and repopulated it with people from Italy and Asia, many of them freed slaves. The city quickly rebuilt and prospered again, and by the time Paul arrived, Corinth was the biggest city in Greece, enormously wealthy, and bustling with a mix of people from all over the Mediterranean world.

The city of Corinth that Paul came to in about 45 C.E. shared some surprising similarities with our modern cities. It was a big city for those times, with perhaps as many as three quarters of a million inhabitants, densely packed into a small area. Commerce was the foundation of its great wealth, and wealth was the foundation of social status. It was a city full of newcomers; no family had been there more than three generations, and most had come more recently than that. It was a Roman colony with Roman-style government, yet the culture was highly diverse with people, languages, and religions from all around the Mediterranean. Think of New York at the beginning of the twentieth century, or London at the time of the Industrial Revolution, or Rio de Janeiro today. Corinth in the middle of the first century C.E. was a city of hustle and bustle and wealth, but it had no clear, unifying, deeply rooted religious and cultural base. It was filled with people who had come to make a new life for themselves or who had been brought there by others. It was a city very open to new religious movements, and the Christian movement was probably one of many.

Christian Households in Corinth

Christians in Corinth met in someone's house, yet it would be somewhat misleading to call these gatherings house churches. That terminology implies that other kinds of churches existed, but they did not. Other religious groups generally had a temple or a sacred place or an assembly hall of some kind, but Christians had access only to some particular person's space. The general word for a Christian gathering was *ekklesia,* which could be translated as "assembly" and was a secular term for any group that had been called to meet for a purpose.

A Roman house was a one- or two-story block of rooms built around an open space; it would probably look like a small apartment building to us. The family and their slaves and servants had sleeping rooms, living quarters, and reception rooms, and there might be some other relatives or

tenants living in the house as well. The family business
was run out of the house, so there would be offices and
perhaps workshops and a store. Other businesses usually
rented space for shops on the noisy street side, and maybe
a tavern or inn would occupy part of the ground floor. All
of these people were part of the household and their families and clients and business partners could be included
as well.

What bound this diverse group together was the relationship of dependence on the head of the household for
protection and patronage. Some of the people were family,
of course, but many were related simply as clients to their
patron. From Paul's letters and from other sources, it seems
that Corinthian households had more diverse patterns than
those in a tradition-bound city like Rome, where the lines
of authority and patronage had been established for generations. In Corinth, not only did females, such as Chloe,
head households, but in some households the husband and
wife seemed to function equally as the head, like the household of Prisca and Aquila, Paul's friends. "Household" is a
much larger concept than family, since it includes a diversity of social classes and occupations.

The household was the basic unit of society and also
the basic form of church in the first century, and this structure strongly influenced how Christians saw themselves
and how they lived out their faith. For one thing, a house
can only take in a few extra people for a meeting—perhaps
15 or 20—and so as the Christian movement grew in
Corinth, it developed a cluster of household groups rather
than one larger community. Paul sees the various household groups as part of one Corinthian *ekklesia,* but potential for conflict was built into such an arrangement.

The other major influence of the household on the new Christian movement was the tendency to simply transfer its social structure into the church. Sometimes this seemed like a gift, sometimes a challenge, and sometimes a perversion—and sometimes it was hard to tell which was which. On the plus side, at least from a practical point of view, the custom was that the household followed its head. If the head of the household was converted to Christianity, it was likely that the whole household would be baptized and space and other resources would be offered to the church. However, we can tell that the household was not always unified in its conversion, because Paul needs to address this question as he counsels believers married to unbelievers to remain in the marriage, unless the unbeliever initiates a divorce (7:12-16).

More problematic was the tension between the authority of the head of the household and the equality in Christ of all baptized believers. The divisions and widely different practices among the households in Corinth were possible because households were independent units where the head made the rules. Different households championed different founders—Paul, Apollos, and Christ—and had varying understandings of sexual morality. Heads of households could not meet together to discuss these differences because there was no higher structure. Some people, such as Paul himself, were generally recognized as having teaching authority, yet this recognition was not permanent or uncontested.

Was the head of the household to be automatically considered the head of the congregation meeting in his house? Clearly not, as far as Paul was concerned. Paul pushed for a radical equality in the life of the church—neither slave nor free, Jew nor Gentile, male nor female. However, household churches evidently found it difficult to let go of such basic social distinctions. How could the head of the household acknowledge that one of his slaves had been given the gift of leadership, while his only gift was to provide the space and pay the bills? You can imagine the difficulties. Some of the problems Paul addresses in his letters arise from confusion between gifts of the Spirit and gifts given by wealth and social status.

The Trouble in Corinth

One thing we know for sure is that there were major problems in the assembly at Corinth. Paul begins strategically with a strong assertion of his own authority and a firm reminder to the Corinthian Christians of their place in the whole assembly of Christians. "Paul, called [*kletos*] to be an apostle of Christ Jesus by the will of God, and our brother Sosthenes, To the church [*ekklesia*] of God that is in Corinth, to those who are sanctified in Christ Jesus, called [*kletois*] to be saints, together with all those who in every place call on the name of our Lord Jesus Christ, both their Lord and ours" (1 Cor. 1:1–2). Paul continues on a note of lavish praise, giving thanks for the Corinthians' great wisdom and spiritual gifts. Perhaps there is already a bit of sarcasm in his words, but more likely, he feels a need to open in a friendly way, since he has no formal authority to command a hearing from them.

But once the opening pleasantries are out of the way, it is immediately clear that Paul is upset with the church he planted in Corinth. His tone ranges from dismay to disgust as he enumerates a series of problems he has heard about:

- There is division, jealousy, and quarreling among them. (1:11; 3:3)
- The Corinthians are immature Christians. (3:2)
- They boast about their spiritual gifts. (4:7)
- They are arrogant about their knowledge. (4:18)
- At least one of their members is guilty of scandalous sexual immorality. (5:1)
- The whole community is guilty of tolerating immorality. (5:11)
- Believers are appealing to outsiders to judge between them. (6:5)
- Some forget that the human body is holy and a member of Christ. (6:15)
- Some couples practice a false asceticism, denying each other conjugal rights. (7:3)
- Some falsely seek spiritual benefit by changing their marital status. (7:17)
- Some are thoughtless toward brothers and sisters who worry about eating food offered to idols. (8:4, 12)
- Women are leading worship with their heads uncovered. (11:5)
- Wealthier Christians humiliate the poor at the Lord's table. (11:22)
- They are keen to rank spiritual gifts as more and less important. (12:16)
- They have forgotten that the only "more important" gift is love. (13:13)
- They are overly fond of speaking in tongues, which is all very well but does not build up the community. (14:4)

- Some are denying the reality of the resurrection of Christ and of believers. (15:17)

The list is impressive—if that is the right word! The Corinthian Christians seem to be wandering all over the place. Doctrinal problems, moral problems, cultural problems—all add up to chaos in the community. There is no common thread to these problems; in fact, they are often contradictory. For instance, some of the Christians apparently believe that the freedom of the gospel gives them license to do anything, including sexual acts that would formerly have been considered immoral. On the other hand, some of the Christians believe that denying the body, particularly repressing sexual urges, even within marriage, is a superior form of spirituality.

The household structure plays a role in all these problems. Each household tends to act independently, so one group claims to follow Apollos and another Cephas, and one group is acting out sexually while another is practicing asceticism. The cultural diversity of this old-new city also plays a role. Some of the Corinthian Christians, and Paul as well, are scandalized at the very idea of women leading worship with their heads uncovered, but apparently some cultures represented in Corinth find it quite normal. Some behaviors, such as eating meat offered to idols, cannot easily be labeled right or wrong, but others, such as eating all the food at the Lord's supper before some of the poorer believers have arrived, are absolutely unacceptable in the Christian community. But how can one distinguish between essentials and nonessentials? Paul's major concern is the divisions and quarrels in the *ekklesia*, and he frequently appeals for unity, but how can they be united in such a diverse city, in their different households?

Paul Responds to the Problems in Corinth

Those of us who work and worship in twenty-first century churches, which sometimes also have problems, should sympathize with Paul. He has almost none of the resources that we can take for granted when our churches are troubled or divided. Consider his predicament: he cannot tell the Corinthians to obey "The Book of Discipline" or "The Manual" or canon law. He can't tell them to follow the prayer book or to consider what the theologians have said about this or that. He can't promise to send them a consultant from the presbytery or threaten to remove their minister. None of these possibilities existed.

In the middle of the first century c.e., what we have come to think of as tradition was still a living and growing body of knowledge circulating orally in different forms, and the only "Bible" was the collection of Hebrew scriptures. The very concept of church was just beginning to take shape, and standards of doctrine, worship, and polity had not been formed. No *church* could be found in Corinth, not only in the sense that there were no church buildings, but also in the sense that nothing quite like what we recognize as church existed. Many other religions had temples in the city, but Christians had none. Christians met in houses, yet they were not simply another social or business gathering such as the head of the household would have. Fraternal organizations often met in people's houses for dinners, but fraternal organizations did not have the wide social mix found in Christian groups. Corinth had synagogues, but Christians of Gentile origin, especially the women, were not fully welcomed there. All of these different social patterns found in Corinth influenced the Christian church that was coming into being, yet none of them was quite adequate to the task of providing a structure for the community of the Risen Lord. Paul was forced to articulate something new, a new identity for a new kind of *ekklesia,* a community founded on the good news about Jesus Christ.

A New Identity for a New Community

Paul's new and astonishing identity for the Christian community in Corinth is this: "You are the body of Christ" (12:27). He arrives at this conclusion in good Greek fashion, meandering around, adding bits and pieces to his argument until the conclusion is inescapable. Or perhaps he is thinking out his argument as he dictates his letter! In any case, there are three distinct parts to Paul's reflections on the church in 1 Corinthians 12. First, Paul says the *ekklesia* is a body and all the Corinthian Christians are members of it. Second, Paul says that each member has been given a gift by the Spirit, and all the gifts working properly together are needed to build up the body and keep it healthy. Third, Paul says that the body in question is the body of Christ.

Paul begins with the idea that the *ekklesia* is a body. Actually, there is nothing particularly new and astonishing about comparing a social group to a body and the members of the group to the parts of that body. It was a common image in Greek writing (not found in the Hebrew scriptures) for social unity despite individual diversity. The body is a useful metaphor that allows Paul to appeal for unity among the fractious Corinthians. A body works together in a coordinated fashion because all the parts submit to a common purpose. Parts cannot run off on their own, and if any part is injured, the whole body suffers. So far, Paul's argument is rather obvious, and is clearly directed at the problems of disunity among the Christian households in Corinth.

Paul gives this image an interesting twist, however, when he adds the idea of spiritual gifts. Again, he is addressing a specific problem raised by the Corinthians. They are apparently arguing about the relative importance of different gifts. Paul wants to remind them that each gift of the Spirit, like each member of the body, has a place. Each member, he says, is given a particular gift: "To each is given the manifestation of the Spirit for the common good" (12:7). Paul enumerates some of the gifts and concludes, "All these are activated by one and the same Spirit, who allots to each one individually just as the Spirit chooses" (12:11). He goes on in a famous passage to underscore the implication: "If the foot would say to the hand, 'Because I am not a hand, I do not belong to the body,' that would not make it any less a part of the body" (12:15).

The body image is now much more sharply focused. We are no longer talking about body as an image of unity for addressing the *problem* of individual diversity. Now we are talking about unity in a *necessary* diversity, where each member has a God-given, Spirit-activated gift essential for the well-being of the body. Paul shifts our focus from the body as a whole to the individual parts as necessary in their specific roles, all the while maintaining the idea of unity. The ideal is not for everyone to become the same or to achieve the same level. Difference is not a problem, but an essential part of unity. And unity is not only, not even primarily, the result of the members' intention to cooperate: unity is a gift of the Spirit who has given just the right gift to each of the members to make the body.

By shifting focus this way, Paul can challenge the Corinthians' divisive and arrogant behavior. Body parts don't get to choose their roles, and cutting yourself off, or cutting others off, is a foolish idea. Fights among body parts would be nonsensical. God has made our bodies so "that there may be no dissension within the body, but the members may have the same care for one another. If one member suffers, all suffer together with it; if one member is honored, all rejoice together with it" (12:25-26). This is what the Christian *ekklesia* is supposed to be like—a body with all its parts working together smoothly. When one is not healthy, the whole community is concerned, and when one works especially well, the whole community is honored. Since the Spirit has given all the various gifts, they all have a place and a purpose, and conflict between them needs to be resolved within the community, for surely this is what the Spirit intends. You could say that the body that is the church is made up of gifts working together, as much as members working together.

At this point in Paul's argument, the body image is a rather heavy challenge, but Paul has more to say. He puts the keystone in place with the amazing statement, "Now you are the body of Christ and individually members of it." With these words, Paul shifts the body image to a whole new level. The image of the body, even when it is focused on individual members as necessary parts of the body, could be applied to any social group (at least, any social group that wished to place a high value on diversity within unity). But the Christians in Corinth, Paul says, are not like just any human body. They are a particular body, the body of Christ. We have stepped out of the realm of social analogies and into the realm of faith. To say that a church is like a body and all the members are valuable is not particularly new, although it is a useful image. But to say that the church in Corinth is the body of Christ is not only new, it is good news for this church and for all churches. Paul has forged a new identity for the Christian *ekklesia* in Corinth, and I believe it remains the core identity for all Christian communities to this day.

Being the Body of Christ

It is easy for us to miss the power of Paul's affirmation, "You are the body of Christ." It has become something of a cliché over the centuries, and my impression is that people often hear it as a statement about the church-in-general and certainly not about their congregation. Perhaps, if pushed, people would say something like, "Well, maybe *your* church is the body of Christ, but *mine* doesn't measure up!" Yet Paul does not, I think, intend to lay another burden on the Corinthians but to lay a foundation for the life of the community. He simply states a fact: "You are the body of Christ."

In our brief journey through Paul's first letter to the Corinthians, we have seen how sad, disgusted, and angry he is with this church. Everything they do is wrong it seems, and Paul lets them know in no uncertain terms that they are a pretty miserable bunch. And yet, it is to these very same Corinthians that Paul says, "You are the body of

Christ!" I think of some of the sad, bad, and mad congregations I have known, the ones that get whispered about in
clergy gatherings, the ones whose lay leaders weep at night
for the pain of it all, and I hear Paul saying to each one of
them, "You are the body of Christ." And I think of the strong
and healthy churches, small and large, in big cities and at
rural crossroads, and I hear Paul say to each one of them,
too, "You are the body of Christ." This is the starting point,
the rock-bottom irreducible identity of the local church. It
is a matter of faith, the assumption we can begin with.

Now Paul's apparently meandering reflections on body
and spiritual gifts spring into sharp focus. The local church
or congregation is the body of Christ, and the Spirit has
given each member gifts that are all to be used for the common good, for building up the body. The church in Corinth,
and every church, has been given all the gifts it needs
and needs all the gifts it has been given in order to live as
the body of Christ. This is Paul's new foundation for all local churches. It is a beginning theology of the Church,
starting from the congregation, from the real life of Christian communities. More is needed, of course, and more
was added over the centuries in various streams of the
tradition, but it is a wonderful starting place for every
congregation.

Saying that a congregation is the body of Christ is like
saying that an individual person is made in the image of
God: we are naming a permanent state of being, not an
achievement or a possession that could be gained or lost.
Such a state of being is not visible with the physical eye,
yet it has a profound effect on how we think of ourselves
and others and the world around us. When we can deeply
acknowledge that we ourselves are made in the image of

God, we feel both the dignity of our status in the world and the challenge to live up to it. Looking at, thinking about, acting towards the other people around us—we are aware that they are made in the image of God, too. Even when a person is difficult or hurtful we know that they are made in the image of God, and we cannot be indifferent to their suffering. The state of being made in the image of God is both a comfort and a challenge.

For a congregation to see itself as the body of Christ can be enormously comforting and challenging, too. I am reminded of the well-known story, "The Rabbi's Gift." This story has appeared in many versions in many places,[2] but here is a short version. An old monastery has declined to the point that it is clearly dying. Once it was a thriving institution with many members, but now the community consists of only four elderly monks and their equally elderly abbot. The brothers are depressed and angry, crotchety with each other, and ashamed of what they have become.

The abbot goes to visit an old rabbi who lives nearby and asks him if he has any advice for this failing monastery. The rabbi says no, he can't think of anything helpful, but he does know, "One of you is the Messiah." The abbot goes back to the monastery and shares this peculiar statement with the brothers, but none of them can figure out what it means. The old rabbi must be crazy! When they consider their pathetic little remnant community, they are sure that none of *them* could possibly be the Messiah. But just on the off chance that the rabbi knows something they don't, they begin to look at each other with a kind of affectionate curiosity that gradually becomes respect and then eventually love. They begin to treat each other as if the other was indeed the Messiah.

A chance visitor notices the lovely serenity that enfolds this tiny community now and tells some friends. The news spreads, and people begin to visit the monastery just to experience this holy love. Soon, some decide to join the community, and gradually, the monastery is restored to vibrant life.

"The Rabbi's Gift" reminds us how the way we think of ourselves in relation to God can have a powerful effect on our other relationships. It is a time-worn phrase but nevertheless true to say that we are called to be Christ for one another and to see Christ in one another. But what would happen if we began to shape our lives according to this profound truth? This is the question the story asks. And I ask, what would it be like for a congregation to know deep in its heart that it *is* the body of Christ? Not that it *should* be the body of Christ (but it isn't), nor that it *could* be the body of Christ (if only it tried harder or had more members or more money), but simply that it *is* the body of Christ, just as it is. I believe that the implications are profound and extensive.

Just as the elderly monks in the story begin to treat each other in a new way because it might be that one of them is the Messiah, so we look at a congregation in a different way if we think it is the body of Christ. A different way of thinking about the congregation leads to a different attitude and practice—a different spirituality. If we believe that each of the members of our congregation is a part of Christ's body with an important gift to contribute, then we find ourselves looking at them with curiosity and respect— even the members we thought of as problems, the ones we secretly or not so secretly wished would go away. And we can't say anymore that we could be a good church if we could just revive the youth group, or get more members,

or fire the organist. We are already the body of Christ—
what more do we need to be faithful in our common
ministry?

We may also think about the implications of being the
body of Christ in the world. Our primary model for Christ
in the world is Jesus and his life and work, and his death
and resurrection. When we consider what we know about
Jesus's actions and relationships with his world, we wonder if we are using our gifts in the right way. The image of
the body of Christ takes us well beyond the values of cohe-
siveness and cooperation within the church, important as
these are. Given what we know about Jesus's bodied exist-
ence, some kinds of activities seem more appropriate than
others (maybe even required!), and some activities are simply excluded. For example, even though we could raise a
lot of money for good purposes, we really can't set the
church up as a brothel or a casino. When we look at what
Jesus did, we can see that the body of Christ is called to
care for the hungry, the sick, and the oppressed—to an-
nounce, point to, and demonstrate the reign of God.

The image of the body of Christ also carries within it a
sharp critique of our North American worship of consum-
erism and success. Faithfulness to God may not bring comfort and prosperity to us, any more than Jesus enjoyed
luxury and fame. Faithfully living as the body of Christ may
bring criticism, hardship, and even death—all these were
experienced by Jesus, after all—and of course we are
daunted by the idea of suffering for our faith. Nevertheless, the body of Christ was resurrected to new life, and
this promise, if it was taken seriously in the church, would
give our congregations the courage to let go of the need to
succeed. There is no promise that being the body of Christ
in the world will be easy.

I hope that some comfortable, successful churches, awakening to a new sense of themselves as the body of Christ, might begin to wonder if they are living up to their full potential. Have they found all the gifts, much less put them all to work as the Spirit intends? Have they clothed this body of Christ with clothes that belong to some other kind of body? Do they look more like a social club or a self-help group? Would the community around them point to them and say, "That's the body of Christ?" Have they invested so carefully in their security that there is no chance they will ever experience suffering and death, much less resurrection? What does it mean for a "successful" congregation to be the body of Christ? What is life abundant for the body of Christ? Comfortable churches may hear more challenge than reassurance in the knowledge that they are the body of Christ.

However, there are many more uncomfortable churches than comfortable ones. For these churches, the fact that they are the body of Christ is good news indeed. Think of all the small and getting smaller churches who fear they are going to die, all the churches buffeted by demographic changes who are bewildered at the loss of their neighborhood, and all the churches consumed by conflicts who know they are behaving badly but can't see their way out. Think of all the churches shaken by the end of Christendom and their church's accustomed role in society. All of these churches need to find their foundation again, so they can continue their ministry with confidence.

A congregation takes a big step forward when it realizes that this particular congregation is the body of Christ, just as it is right now, but this step is not the end of the road. After we have sung a heartfelt chorus of "Just as I am, without one plea,"[3] we do have to make some decisions and get on with life. As we sit in the pews of our particular church, we know in faith that our congregation is the body of Christ and that the Holy Spirit has given us all the gifts we need to be who we are, but what are our particular gifts and what ministry in particular is ours? The body of Christ takes on many shapes and forms. What is ours?

Identity with Pride

The following story tells what happens when a congregation that is beginning to get confused about its ministry in the world explores what it means to be the body of Christ in its own particular way.

South Valley Church is in a new suburb and is quite new itself. It was started about 10 years ago when the houses were going up like mushrooms and the streets weren't even paved. The church has grown rapidly, and the new sanctuary is filled every Sunday. The congregation is made up almost exclusively of young couples with one or two young children. In a typical family, both parents work long hours and have their children in day care. Families have very limited time and money, but they really love their church and contribute generously. Things have settled down a bit from the first years of rapid growth, although the congregation is still growing. Money is always a problem, but so far the congregation is making the budget and chipping away at the mortgage.

Yet there is a kind of uneasiness in the congregation, a sort of "what now?" feeling. The first few years were such a mad scramble, with all the new people and the building project and getting a basic organizational structure going, that no one had much time to think. But now there is a lot of discussion about getting better organized and finding a focus. Some people have been pushing for a more evangelical style of worship, and some want to take on a major mission project in the community. People have such different ideas. Where does South Valley go from here?

And so the board and as many others who could come gathered to talk about all this one Saturday morning at a nearby church. The muffins were tasty, the singing was hearty, and the consultant invited to work with them for the day seemed promising, so they settled down with goodwill. First, they worshiped, focused on 1 Corinthians 12. This was familiar territory for most of the group because the board had been doing a Bible study on 1 Corinthians since the fall, and the minister had recently preached several sermons on the Corinthian church. They all responded to the prayer petitions firmly and with real conviction, "South Valley Church is the body of Christ."

Then the consultant asked them to try to imagine what kind of body South Valley was. After all, bodies come in all shapes and sizes, all races and social conditions and states of health. So, if they had to imagine South Valley as a particular body, what would that person be like? Which gender, about how old, what occupation, what state of health and fitness? What would be the life challenges and dilemmas of such a person?

They broke into their table groups and began to discuss this interesting question. There was lots of laughter and energy and when the consultant called them back, it seemed too soon. Surprisingly, they had all come up with basically the same image. They all agreed that South Valley was sort of like a teenaged boy, about 13 years old.

Some of the qualities and characteristics that came up included the following:

- Boundless energy, but could fall asleep for long periods
- Great enthusiasm, but not such great organization
- Terrific at short-term projects, but easily bored if anything went on too long
- Growing out of his pants every few months
- Voice wobbling up and down
- Wide-eyed and open-hearted

Everyone laughed in recognition. How amazing that they had all come up with the same image! Maybe they were onto something! They decided to call this wonderful person Eddie.

So what challenges and opportunities faced Eddie, the consultant asked, and what did he need to flourish—and what should he do with his life? What does a healthy, middle-class, 13-year-old boy need? "Room to grow," someone said, "and lots of interesting opportunities to explore." "He needs to go to school, to learn more. He needs structure and protection—he's still just a kid!" "He needs food," the mother of one of the few teenagers in the congregation said. "He needs someone to get him up on time, to organize him," a teacher said. "He needs lots of love and care and attention, so he will grow up into a fine man." "Into the fullness of the stature of Christ," someone quoted.

Then the consultant asked, if South Valley is like Eddie, what does that suggest to you about the future? There was lots of discussion. One person said, "If we really are like Eddie, it's too soon to take responsibility for that major mission project. We're not ready for it." The chair of the administration committee said, "This confirms our impression that we need to increase the secretary's hours. We really need strong administrative backup for our busy people." The chair of the board said, "I really like Eddie—I think he's great! It seems to me that we're on the right track with our present and rather chaotic style. I get impatient with it sometimes, but Eddie needs lots of freedom to try different things." When the chair of the board finished, everyone applauded.

The discussion continued in the parking lot and into the months ahead as South Valley came to a whole new sense of pride in its identity as the body of Christ, otherwise known as Eddie.

3

Who Are We Really?

The congregation named Eddie came to an image of itself as the body of Christ quickly and easily, but in my experience, getting to a realistic sense of identity is a richer and more complex process. In this chapter, we walk through the personal identity exercise with a congregation, paying attention to the whole journey. The chapter concludes with a brief story of another type of congregation working out its own particular way of being the body of Christ.

Getting Ready for the Annual Meeting at St. Mark's

The young adults group was setting out the chairs and tables in the Christian education hall while the men's breakfast club made sandwiches and the Martha unit started the coffee and set out trays of cookies and squares. The choir was rehearsing the hymns, and the children were practicing the song they were going to lead. Lots of noise,

cheerful voices, the smell of coffee, kids running around—
St. Mark's Church was getting ready for the annual meeting of the congregation.

"Sure is different from last year," Brad said, as he kicked
the legs open on another table and locked them into place.
"I guess," said Jennifer. "I didn't come last year. Just couldn't
face another fight." "You and most of the congregation,"
Brad agreed. "But look at us now! How many of these darn
tables do we need, anyway? Do you think we will really get
65 people out for an annual meeting?" In the kitchen, George
was asking the same question. "How many sandwiches do
we need? Personally, I think it was a mistake trying to put
worship and lunch and the meeting all together. I think
people will stay away in droves! We only get about a hundred people out on a regular Sunday. Reverend Thompson's
crazy if he thinks he'll get 65 to stay for the annual general
meeting!" "Oh, George, quit your grumbling and finish those
sandwiches," Elsie said. "We've phoned the whole list, and
almost everyone says they're coming."

Meanwhile, Bill Thompson gathered with the board in
the library. They reviewed the plans for the meeting. The
worship was to be brief and light-hearted, with a focus on
1 Corinthians 12, of course. The children would close by
leading them all in the action song, "The Living Church"[1]
and then go downstairs for a special program led by the
youth group from a neighboring church. The adults and
youth would continue with the business meeting, which
would be brief and uncontroversial, the board hoped. After the business meeting, they would go into the "personal
identity exercise," as Bill called it. The board members had
gone over the exercise several times, and they would
spread themselves around all the tables so they could help

keep their group on track. They were all excited and a bit nervous: What if no one came? What if it didn't work? Simon, the chair of the board, led them in a prayer for the presence and guidance of the Spirit. For the first time in years, the board members were happy and hopeful about their church, and they longed for the whole congregation to experience that same sense of renewal.

The Trouble at St. Mark's

Bill flipped through the annual report as he took a few minutes to focus before the service. St. Mark's was in pretty good shape: attendance was back to the same level as three years ago, and the deficit would probably be eliminated this year. The congregation had regained its confidence and a spirit of health and energy. Bill and the lay leaders had focused for the past year on healing and rebuilding, and the work had born good fruit. Bill thought about the state of the congregation a year ago and winced: St. Mark's had certainly been through a painful period!

Up to three years ago, St. Mark's had been a healthy congregation with about 100 members. The congregation had had strong and effective leadership and had weathered the declines of the '60s and '70s very well. The older generation had gracefully let go of the power positions and handed over the leadership to a younger group. In fact, St. Mark's had become that comparative rarity, a boomer congregation. Much of this healthy evolution took place with the guidance of Rev. Matthew Smith. During his 10-year pastorate, Matt brought out the best in the congregation while he continued to grow and develop in his own ministry. Matt and his wife and children were at the center of St.

Mark's, loved by everyone. After 10 years, Matt accepted a
call to a larger church in another part of the country, and
the congregation celebrated his ministry and said good-
bye to the family.

The congregation moved quickly to call Rev. Dorothy
Evans. Dorothy looked like the leader they needed for the
future. She was an engaging and creative worship leader
and an immediate hit with the youth. Although the congregation was still in shock at Matt's rather sudden departure, they liked Dorothy, and her pastorate started well.
Then the trouble began.

The first problem had nothing to do with Dorothy. Only
a few months after Matt left, people were shocked to hear
that Matt and his wife were divorcing. Apparently Matt was
leaving his wife for another woman and was going to marry
again very quickly. Matt's wife and teenaged children turned
to their old friends at St. Mark's for sympathy and support,
and there was a steady flow of upsetting information. The
congregation was devastated. The teenagers, who had
grown up with Matt's children, were particularly angry. How
could everyone have been so wrong about Matt? All the
members were confused and hurt, but they didn't know
what to do. The revelations troubled everyone, and members were divided over whether they should have seen it
coming and done something, or whether it was really none
of their business since Matt was gone. No one talked to
Dorothy about this situation, because there was nothing
she could do about it, and anyway, they thought, she
shouldn't be burdened with something the previous minister did. An uncomfortable silence covered an uproar of
gossip.

Less than a year after Dorothy arrived, some members
of the congregation, especially the leaders, began to feel

uneasy about her ministry. The personnel committee was hearing complaints about Dorothy being late for meetings or not present at all. The worship committee was frustrated that Dorothy never seemed to plan her services but just pulled them out of her head at the last minute. The secretary threatened to resign, because Dorothy was hardly ever in the church office and sometimes didn't get the information for the Sunday bulletin to her until Friday noon. On the other hand, most of the congregation really appreciated Dorothy's informal worship style and thought she was a good pastor in crisis situations. The youth really loved her. The board asked the personnel committee to work with Dorothy to help her be better organized. They gave her a Palm Pilot for Christmas.

The personnel committee met with Dorothy. She was contrite: she said she realized her working style was not the best, she wanted to apologize for her disorganization, and she would definitely do better. There was some improvement for a brief time, but then Dorothy's behavior returned to the former pattern. The personnel committee was now getting complaints from all sides. They spoke to Dorothy again and gave her concrete guidelines for some areas of her work. Dorothy was insulted and reminded them that St. Mark's had called her because she was a creative free spirit. The personnel committee felt they were out of their depth; everything they did to get Dorothy to behave better seemed to backfire on them. They called in a consultant from the judicatory who made recommendations that neither Dorothy nor the congregation seemed able to follow.

Dorothy had built a loyal following in the congregation, and these members felt that she was being persecuted because she was a woman or that the old guard were just trying to make her be well organized like Matt. The board instructed the personnel committee to settle these problems with Dorothy, and the whole personnel committee resigned. The new personnel committee, a careful balance of pro-Dorothy and anti-Dorothy members, deadlocked in an argument about whether to hire a full-time administrator or to terminate Dorothy's appointment.

The conflict deepened until the whole congregation was painfully involved. Some members of the board resigned. Sunday attendance dropped sharply, and some of the largest givers withheld their offerings. The chair of the board called the judicatory, and after an investigation, Dorothy was removed and placed on medical leave. The judicatory officials could not say anything about Dorothy's departure, citing medical confidentiality rules. Dorothy never came back.

The judicatory arranged pulpit supply for St. Mark's, and there was an immediate sense of relief. Yet, the conflict was not over. Now everyone was criticizing everyone else about their actions during Dorothy's short, unhappy time with them. The conflict had strained and broken relationships in the congregation. Harsh words had been spoken, and it was hard to forgive and trust again. The congregation was resentful of the judicatory's actions in removing its minister and unsatisfied with the lack of explanation. Members were frightened that, twice in a row, they had been so wrong about the minister they had chosen, and their confidence was badly shaken. Instead of calling a new minister for a long-term pastorate, they contracted with Bill Thompson, a retired minister, to work with them for two years. They wanted someone who would be steady and gentle with them and who wouldn't give them any nasty surprises.

When Bill arrived, he found the congregation divided and demoralized. However, his gentle pastoral wisdom was just what was needed, and gradually the congregation was restored to health. A few members still couldn't let go of the arguments about Dorothy, but most of the people had moved on and could say that they had just been unlucky to have two such strange and difficult experiences with their ministers. In liturgy and small-group discussions, people were able to acknowledge their hurt and anger, and ask each other for forgiveness and understanding. They were ready to look at the future.

As part of the healing process and also in preparation for the future, Bill reflected with the congregation on the nature of ministry and the congregation's ways of relating to its clergy leader. Bill knew they were anxious about choosing their next minister and wanted them to feel confident that they could take responsibility for the ministry of their church and not leave it all up to the ordained person. He reminded them that, in order to choose a new minister and build a healthy relationship with him or her, they needed to know who they were and where they were going. Bill led them in Bible study and worship about being the body of Christ, and now he was about to lead them in the next step: focusing on their particular way of being the body of Christ.

Bill picked up his notes and headed for the Christian education hall.

Who Is St. Mark's?

The noise in the CE hall was beginning to die down. Everyone found a chair around the tables and began to sing the first hymn. The mood was rather solemn as Bill reflected on the journey of the past year and reminded them of the pain and confusion in which they had begun. But by the time the children had led them in the action song and trooped noisily down to the basement with the youth group from the other church, everyone was relaxed and eager to get going. A quick headcount revealed just over 70 adults staying for the meeting, so Bill and the board members made sure there were 10 tables and firmly directed the congregation to sit with seven or eight at each table.

The business part of the meeting went as smoothly as the board had hoped. The news was mostly good (very good, compared to last year), and enthusiastic thanks were offered to the board and Bill. The budget was straightforward and passed with just a few questions. Simon, the chair of the board, explained that longer-term plans, including the process for calling a new minister, would depend in part on the work they were going to do today. He talked about the board's hopeful enthusiasm, so the lunch break was filled with a buzz of anticipation.

Bill began by telling stories about other churches that had done this personal identity exercise. He told them about a church that saw itself as a teenager named Eddie, and about a church that called itself Sarah because, although she was an old woman, she seemed pregnant with new life. He told them about a church that saw herself as an elderly woman coming to the end of her life who wanted to leave a good legacy. The churches Bill described were nothing like St. Mark's, and perhaps because of that, the members began to understand how each church was distinct and could be seen as a single person. When Bill could feel that most of the room was with him, he explained the process for the rest of the day.

They would begin by describing the person they imagined St. Mark's to be. They would have about 20 minutes for this task in their table groups. Each table included a board member who would help them keep on track and remember their "holy manners." The board member also had a sheet with some questions on it and would write up notes, and after the table groups had done their work, each table group would report to the whole gathering. The questions on the sheet included the following:

Which gender?
About how old?
What does he/she look like? (general appearance, style, clothes)
What does he/she do? (occupation, lifestyle, hobbies)
What is his/her state of health and fitness?
What is his/her life setting? (recent events, new challenges and opportunities)
What is his/her favorite TV show and radio station?
What does he/she eat for breakfast?
If you had to introduce him/her to a friend, what would you say?

Bill explained that the questions were really just to spark their imagination and that there were no incorrect answers. It didn't matter if the groups answered all the questions—they should just enjoy working on them.

When Bill finished speaking, conversations sprang up at all the tables. The noise level rose to a roar and then settled as the groups got to work. Bill wandered around the room, listening to the conversations, ready to coach if necessary. Several of the table groups had trouble focusing on the task. George was grumbling that he didn't see the point of the whole thing. As far as he was concerned St. Mark's just needed to call its new minister and get on with life. At another table, one member of the group seemed to want to rehash the whole controversy about Rev. Dorothy. A couple of tables were having trouble getting into a playful, right-brain mode and were analyzing the congregation instead of developing an image. The board members were coping well with all the questions, however, and Bill began to relax. Most of the table groups had jumped in eagerly, and their energy was beginning to carry the room. By the time Bill called out to say they had only 15 minutes left, the few tables that were still not fully engaged looked around and decided they had better get to work.

With five minutes remaining, Bill had to shout to make himself heard over the cheerful noise, and when he called out, "Time! Wrap it up!" groans of disappointment filled the room. Now, Bill explained, each table group was going to report, and they would all listen. He suggested that each group try to limit itself to five minutes at most. Bill took care to call on some of the strongest groups first, knowing that the others would be refining their reports as they listened.

Jennifer reported for the first table, and her excitement and humor engaged everyone. As she reported, one of the members took notes on chart paper and taped the sheets up on the wall. Jennifer's report looked like this:

Which gender?
more female than male

About how old?
40-ish

What does he/she look like?
>   *nice-looking, casual style, likes to wear good jeans*
>   *(not the $400 ones, but not the $25 ones, either)*
>   *doesn't wear a lot of makeup*
>   *dresses up occasionally, for a really good night out*

What does he/she do?
>   *stay-at-home mom with several kids, but professionally*
>   *trained*
>   *middle class, comfortably off, but not wealthy*
>   *active in community groups, especially around*
>   *children's and women's issues*
>   *likes to sing in a choir and eat with friends*

What is his/her state of health and fitness?
>   *gained a few pounds recently but has been working*
>   *at fitness*
>   *recovering from a time of stress and depression, but*
>   *generally in good health*

What is his/her life setting?
>   *been through a painful divorce and a few unsuitable*
>   *relationships, but ready to start dating again*
>   *The kids are mostly in their teens, and she's thinking*
>   *about going back to work and is anxious about that.*
>   *middle age looms*

What is his/her favorite TV show and radio station?
>   *soft rock*

What does he/she eat for breakfast?
>   *Who has time for breakfast? Eats the kids' leftovers!*

If you had to introduce him/her to a friend, what would
   you say?
   "Would you like to date my friend? She's really nice!"

Everyone roared with laughter at the last comment. Bill
had trouble getting them to settle down to listen to the
next report. The second table group's flip chart report
looked like this:

Which gender?
   definitely female

About how old?
   45

What does he/she look like?
   attractive, a few grey hairs showing
   likes casual clothes

What does he/she do?
   teacher, very busy juggling career and kids
   spends time with her kids on weekends
   sings in a choir

What is his/her state of health and fitness?
   good, maybe likes to eat too much

What is his/her life setting?
   In the past few years has had to cope with several prob-
      lems "off stage" (like serious illness in the family)
      that have drained her. Hard to get her energy back.

What is his/her favorite TV show and radio station?
likes nature shows and classic rock

What does he/she eat for breakfast?
grabs a bagel as she runs out the door

If you had to introduce him/her to a friend, what would you say?
n/a

Other
perimenopausal

The whole group thought that was pretty funny, too, although some of the men had to have the word explained to them. Bill was amused to see a few red faces among the older men and the teenaged boys. He called on the next table. Their report (clearly influenced by the presence of several youth group members) looked like this:

Which gender?
female

About how old?
39 and holding

What does he/she look like?
cool mom

What does he/she do?
works at home

likes to eat out with friends
goes to sports practices with her kids
very musical

What is his/her state of health and fitness?
good, for her age

What is his/her life setting?
a lot of arguments in the last few years, but more peace-
ful now
needs to find a new partner and get on with her life

What is his/her favorite TV show and radio station?
watches the news and listens to "moldy oldies"

What does he/she eat for breakfast?
n/a

If you had to introduce him/her to a friend, what would
you say?
n/a

As each table group added its report, Bill could feel the
sense of wonder and pleasure growing in the room. The
people of St. Mark's really did know who they were! With
all the different voices and all the particular details, a single
picture was taking shape. The whole group, far from being
bored by the slightly repetitive reports, greeted each new
affirmation of its identity and each new detail about it with
cheers and laughter. Bill listened to it all very carefully.
The exercise was going very well, and it looked as if his
part was going to be fairly straightforward. They took a
stretch and coffee break.

A Portrait of St. Mark's

Bill called the group back and explained that their job now was to put the pictures together into one. He wrote "gender?" on the chart paper. "I think "female" was the clear winner here, although there was some ambiguity. What's that about?" Several people commented that they didn't like the gender stereotyping, although they could see the point. One person said that St. Mark's was female in a twenty-first century way—not just focused on relationship and belonging, but also invested in career and social projects. To general agreement, Bill wrote:

Which gender?
female, twenty-first century style

The age question was also clearly answered, since all the responses fell between 39 and 45 years old. Bill wrote

About how old?
early 40s

The appearance question took more time, but there was a lot of agreement to work with. Bill pointed out that all the tables had said that she liked good quality casual clothes. He asked, "What would a person/church who preferred formal clothes look like?" "Like St. Anne's," someone quipped. (St. Anne's was a neighboring church devoted to precisely performed ritual and rigidly managed meetings.) And Bill asked, "What would a person/church with shabby, dirty clothes be like?" "Like us last year," someone commented. "That's true," Bill said. "We've come a long way. In fact, I note almost all of you found a way to say our

person is attractive, cool, nice looking." Bill began to write
on the chart paper, accepting prompts from the group.

What does she look like?
> *attractive, good haircut (a little grey showing)*
> *neat, casual style clothes (stylish jeans)*
> *not a lot of makeup*
> *can go formal for a really special occasion*
> *a "soft rock" kind of person*

When it came to the occupation question, it seemed that
there were divergent opinions, particularly over whether
she was a stay-at-home mom, but Bill was really good at
drawing out the common threads in what they had said.

What does she do?
> *She has children, mainly in their teens, and is invested*
> *in looking after them.*
> *She has a good education and a profession. (Teacher,*
> *accountant, HR manager were some of the sug-*
> *gestions.)*
> *The issues of work-family balance are important to*
> *her, as she is either working or thinking of going*
> *back to work soon.*
> *She is busy—maybe too busy.*
> *She likes to spend time with her kids, eat with friends,*
> *and sing in a choir.*

The health and fitness question had not sparked much
interest, Bill noted. He took that as a confirmation of the
healing from the conflict and stress of previous years. No
one had mentioned spiritual health, so Bill asked the whole

group about it. A few people made attempts to add something, but one member said, "The truth is, we didn't think
about it. We don't think about it much. Maybe we should?"
That seemed to evoke lots of agreement, so Bill wrote:

What is her state of health and fitness?
> *has recovered from a period of stress and depression*
> *generally in good health, although needs to continue*
> *to work on fitness*
> *needs to think about her spiritual health*
> *needs to take care of herself and make time to eat a*
> *proper breakfast!*

The question about life setting had generated the most
energy. Almost all the table groups had given extensive
answers to this one, and almost all the answers had two
parts, one that focused on the recent troubles, and one
that looked to future decisions. The turmoil from the past
was most often imaged as a marriage breakdown, although
the phrase about bad things happening "off stage" had
prompted strong agreement. As he reviewed the sheets up
on the wall, Bill was intrigued to see how many reports
talked about impending change—children growing up, going back to work, and the memorable "perimenopausal."
He was pleased to see how many imagined the future as
not simply a time to "recover and continue as before," but
as a new stage in life. With much consultation and advice,
Bill wrote:

What is her life setting?
> *divorced a few years ago and still smarting from a*
> *sense of betrayal; next relationship ended in tur-*

*moil and confusion, as partner just disappeared
has basically recovered from the bitterness and depression and is thinking about dating again
She is facing a new stage in life and has many questions: What comes after the kids are grown up?
Should she go back to work or invest more in her
career?
can't just wait and let a new partner decide these
things—needs to find a partner who will go with
her into (gasp!) middle age*

The questions about music preferences and breakfast
had not elicited much interest, so Bill just added a couple
of phrases to the style and health sheets to cover them.
"How would you introduce her? Does she remind you of
anyone? She needs a name." Someone suggested "Perry
M. O'Pawsel" and everyone groaned. "Markette" was too
much like market for everyone's taste. "Debra," Jennifer
said, "because she was a judge in Israel and a strong
woman." Everyone agreed: it seemed just right. Bill wrote:

How would you introduce her?
  Debra
  *Because she was a strong woman and a judge in
  Israel*

Thinking About Debra

"What's it like to be Debra?" Bill asked. "Here she is, a nice-
looking woman in her early 40s, has had some relationships end unhappily but is ready to try again. Her family is

growing up, and a whole new stage in life beckons and threatens. You know, our grandmothers sometimes called menopause 'the change,' or even 'the change in life,' so 'perimenopausal' is a pretty good word for her situation. I wouldn't know, of course, being a 62-year-old man, but I seem to remember that our early 40s was a hard time for my wife. Is it still the same?" Elsie, one of the older ladies, said, "I remember how hard it was for me and a lot of my friends when we went through our 40s. It seemed like the end of so much, with the kids growing up. I wondered what I would do with myself for the rest of my life. But that was years ago! I think it's different now. It seems like a new beginning for a lot of young women." Lisa, who was in her early 40s, said, "That's true in a way, but it still seems like a tough transition. I'm just where Debra is, and I certainly wonder about how good I'll be at a full-time job and how it will feel not to have the kids at home. And then there are all the physical changes."

Bill listened carefully to the conversation. "What you are saying is, our Debra faces important challenges as she moves into middle age, but she seems to be in good shape to make this important transition." Everyone expressed agreement. "What are some of the strengths, the gifts, that Debra has that can help her face the future with confidence? What are her gifts of the Spirit for an abundant life of faithfulness and service?" Bill wrote up the list as they called out suggestions.

She's got enough money.
She has education and a profession, plus all the skills of
*   a good mother.*
Her kids seem okay.

She has a good house with a great location, right by the
  shopping mall.
She is mature, has lots of life experience.
She has learned a lot about men.
She's a survivor, has made it through a rough time.
She's strong, smart, and independent.
She has a good network of friends.
She is respected in the community.

When the group had run out of ideas, Bill wrote down
the next question: "What are some of the things women
like Debra do when they turn 40?" He stood poised to write
as people threw out suggestions.

Start watching your weight and exercise more. It's harder
  to keep fit after 40.
Upgrading and retraining to go back to the workforce.
Develop a new kind of relationship with the kids as they
  become adults.
Think of moving—maybe the house is too big?
Join a book group, take up ballroom dancing—do some-
  thing different!
Think about your spiritual life.
You need to really stop and think about your future. Lots
  of women get scared and jump too fast into a new
  relationship or a new job without really thinking about
  what they need and can do.

The last comment came from Lisa and was greeted with
great respect. It seemed that everyone there knew someone who had made poor choices as they moved into middle
age. Bill reminded them that opportunity and risk go to-

gether, but with God's help, they were going to choose well and wisely. He told them that finding and describing Debra was a beginning step in that process. Now that they had a clear image of who they were, they needed to fill in the details of the portrait and then decide what Debra should do as she moved into middle-age and a new stage of being the body of Christ. He and the board would be asking them to meet again, probably several times, to think about Debra and her future, and he hoped they would respond as generously and work as hard as they had today.

Elsie moved a vote of thanks to Rev. Bill and everyone who had made the meeting such a success. "The best annual meeting I've ever been to, and I've been to a lot!" she said to general applause. Bill led them in a prayer for Debra, and the children came up from the basement to lead them in another round of "The Living Church." The meeting was adjourned to a clatter of chairs and tables and a great buzz of conversation and laughter.

Working with Debra

The board met on the Thursday after the annual meeting, and everyone was eager to talk about the personal identity exercise. Bill said how pleased he was with the experience and thanked the board for its careful work with the table groups. Simon said, "You know, I was a bit skeptical about the whole thing. I mean, I thought it would be fun, but I never imagined we would learn so much!" Most of the board members agreed that it certainly was an upper for the congregation and made everyone feel good, but some didn't think they had learned much. Harry said, "I've been telling people for years that this church was changing.

Remember when I did all those charts on membership and Sunday school attendance? That's all Debra's midlife crisis is about!" Simon responded diplomatically, "You're right, Harry, and I think all your hard work just paid off. Talking about our church in terms of Debra is a way everyone can see and understand the changes you were trying to point out. I was part of the clean-up crew in the kitchen after the meeting, and they sure got the point!"

Bill asked, "What struck you and the people you've been talking to since Sunday?" "I liked the way everyone worked so well together," one of the members said. "And it was just amazing when everyone started to realize that all the groups had come up with almost the same picture." "I was so pleased that we could talk about the troubles of the past few years in a way that made the pain real and yet helped us focus on the future," another said. There was a moment of silence as they all contemplated how far they had come in just a year. "I liked that it was *our* image, that *we* made it. I mean, your role was really important, Bill, but you didn't tell us who we are. You helped us see that we knew already," another added. "Well," said Harry, "I still don't see how Debra really helps us figure out what we should *do!*"

"We'll get there," said Bill. "We have already started, with the last questions I was asking on Sunday. What gifts does Debra have, and what kinds of challenges and options do people like her have? But before we think about what Debra needs to do, we need to make sure that she is a present image in the whole congregation's mind. How are we going to do that?" They brainstormed for a while and came up with a few ideas:

- Have a report about the meeting from a few people on Sunday
- Publish a mini report, especially the description of Debra, in the bulletin every Sunday for the next month
- Publish a full report in the next newsletter

They couldn't think of any other ways of reporting for a few minutes until Brian, who rarely said anything, asked if they would like to see a little sketch of Debra he had drawn on Sunday. He passed around a small piece of paper and everyone saw Debra. There she was, briefcase in one hand, cup of coffee in the other, and a bagel gripped between her teeth. They were delighted, and Brian agreed he could make a larger version, big enough to put up on the wall. In fact, he could imagine a series of drawings. Once the audiovisual possibilities occurred, there was another list:

- Put up Debra's picture on the wall and include it in the newsletter
- Ask the youth group to do a media presentation about Debra and present it to the congregation
- See if the young adult group would like to do a skit about Debra ("Please, no more bad jokes about menopause," Harry grumbled.)
- Ask the choir director to compose a song about Debra

"What about the children?" Bill asked. "How do we keep them involved?" Heather, who taught the seven- and eight-year-old Sunday school class, said she thought the younger children wouldn't really understand the idea of talking about St. Mark's as Debra, but they would like all the audiovisual things. She also thought her class would like to know about Deborah in the Bible. "Kids like hero stories, and Deborah was a mighty leader of Israel. They also like nicknames, and they probably would be pleased to think of Debra as a nickname for St. Mark's." Some people wondered if the story of Deborah was really suitable for small children, but they thought Heather could probably handle it.

Everyone was pleased with the suggestions, and there were volunteers for all the tasks, which was a nice change. Bill cautioned them to remember that this was a long-term project. Certainly, they needed to do a few things right away to solidify the image of Debra in people's minds, but then they would need to refresh the image occasionally in order to keep everyone focused. Simon suggested that the board ensure that there was something planned about once a month, and all agreed that was a good idea. Of course, Bill said, soon there would be new questions about Debra and new details about her life to generate new interest. On that encouraging note, the board went on to the rest of its agenda.

Facing Painful Realities

For some congregations, like St. Paul's in chapter 1 or Dublin Street Church in the following story, facing up to their real identity requires honesty and courage. The personal identity exercise can provide a supportive structure in which to work at identity. Even the toughest situation can produce light-hearted moments.

Dublin Street Church is a mainline Protestant
church built just after the Second World War. It reached its highest membership in the late '50s and has declined steadily ever since. By the year 2000, the end was in sight. Despite the best efforts of the congregation, it seemed certain that they could not continue much longer. They were angry, depressed, and hopeless, and they were convinced that the minister appointed by the judicatory had been sent to close them down, so they were surprised and a little bit encouraged when they were invited to think of other possibilities.

They were sure they were a family church and all they really needed was a young minister with a family to get them going again, but they had to agree that wasn't very likely to happen. When they were invited to include the identity exercise in the annual meeting, the board agreed, as long as it came last on the agenda, so people who didn't want to wouldn't have to stay.

David, the minister appointed to Dublin Street, was not at all sure the identity exercise would work here. He had not been able to train a leadership team, because the congregation was so small and so reluctant to work with him. Only 20 people stayed for the meeting, just enough for four small table groups, and David wondered if the number was sufficient to generate the energy needed to produce a substantial image. One table group was clearly present to keep an eye on what happened, rather than to participate in the exercise. They had a mutinous air about them and talked all through the introductory material on 1 Corinthians. When David set the table groups to work, this group continued to gossip among themselves. The other tables, however, did begin to work on the task, and David heaved a sigh of relief as the rebellious table sensed that they were out of step and started to think about the image.

As 20 minutes went on, the table groups became a little more engaged, and there was even some laughter. David began to breathe easier. The reports from the tables were rather disappointing, however, because the presenters spoke without much energy, and the portrait lacked detail. He was going to have to work hard to get much out of them.

The gender was not in doubt: everyone had said female. The age was disputed. Three of the tables had put her in her 70s or 80s, which seemed quite reasonable to David, but one table said she was only 40. David simply said that that was quite a spread, and asked which one was more accurate. What happened next was fascinating as the group slowly began to grapple with the denial that was such a strong part of the congregation's life. The table that wanted its person to be only 40 was scared to admit that old age was approaching. David asked, "What would be the differences between 40 and 80?" The 40 table, sensing that their position was unreasonable, began to bargain. Maybe she was a senior, they said—maybe 65. The other table groups were kind but firm: this lady was elderly, 75 at least. David was worried about some signs of anger and hurt but was relieved when these were wonderfully resolved after someone shouted out, "She's 80, but she lies about her age!" The tension broke, everyone laughed, and the mood in the room shifted to one of energetic interest.

The appearance and style also seemed uncontroversial. She like stylish casual clothes, although she still wore skirts and hose more often than younger women. (She had only begun wearing pants to church a few years ago.) She liked to keep her hair neatly done and used a little lipstick. She wore sensible shoes. She was a busy senior, and her days were filled with activities at the senior center, church groups, looking after her house, and traveling to visit grandchildren. She used to be involved in the community, and she used to entertain a lot, but she didn't have as much energy as she had back in those days. In fact, she had limited her activities quite a bit in the past few years. She had a few health problems and some arthritis, but she was fiercely independent.

As for her life setting, she lived on her own in her own home. Her children and even her grandchildren were grown up and did not live nearby. They visited now and then, and she visited them, but they were not a daily presence in her life. She loved her house and never wanted to leave it, but it was getting harder for her to look after the property, and she had fallen a couple of times. Her greatest fear was that she would end up in a nursing home. She was just trying to live one day at a time and not worry about the future, but she knew that her present situation couldn't continue much longer.

David was touched by the way working on the image was helping the congregation be so honest about the realities of its situation. The mood was getting quite somber as they talked about the health and housing issue. But laughter broke out again when David asked, "What does she eat for breakfast?" and one person called out, "Bran," and another added, "And pills!"

"Does she have a name?" David asked. They decided to call her "Dubbie" and felt quite affectionate towards her. "What are the important issues for someone like Dubbie?" the minister asked. "What can and should she do?" There were various suggestions: sell the house and move into a condo; take in boarders; divide the house into apartments. (Clearly, the house is a big issue as you get older!) Someone said, "It's important to write a good will, to hand things on to the next generation. After all, when you're in your 80s, you know you won't live forever." A tense silence followed this remark: someone had dared to mention death, the thing they all feared. The next generation had grown up and moved away, and it seemed that death would truly be the end of Dubbie. Slowly, the conversation resumed. Someone commented that if they believed that death was not the end of life, they should not be so afraid to face it. If there was to be new life for Dublin Street Church, they might be able to help it happen, but Dubbie would not likely be there to enjoy it. The meeting closed on that sober note, and David led them in prayer, thanking God for all the years of faithful service of Dublin Street, and asking God for the wisdom and courage to continue in faith, even unto death.

4

Exploring the Personal Identity Exercise

The time has come to step back from the stories and take a more analytic approach to the personal identity exercise. The stories have come first in this book not only because they are engaging for the reader but because they are important tools for leading the exercise in a congregational setting. Nevertheless, a linear way of understanding the personal identity exercise is also useful. The leader of the exercise should have a good grasp of the theory so that he or she can adjust and adapt as necessary. Members of the board or whichever group is going to help lead the exercise may also be interested in knowing the theory that grounds the exercise. In addition, some people (I for one) find it difficult to think of stories as serious learning tools and need to have the theory in hand before they feel comfortable in the less linear medium. In this chapter, we will take a look at how and why the personal identity exercise works and also lay out some of the technical details for conducting the exercise.

Origins of the Personal
Identity Exercise and Why It Works

The first thing to say is, the personal identity exercise does work! I have used it myself about 20 times, and I have been teaching it for several years to clergypersons developing their skills in transitional ministry. Many of these clergy have used the exercise, and all the reports I have heard back are positive. I only know of one situation where it did not work (more about that below), and even there, doing the exercise was instructive. I thought up the basic framework for the exercise 20 years ago when I was serving the first of many interim ministries at a church much like South Valley (see chapter 3). The board had agreed on a planning retreat, and I was looking for an engaging Bible study idea that would support the planning process. Naturally, 1 Corinthians 12 with its image of the body came to mind. I was thinking primarily about the parts of the body and how we might consider each ministry area in the congregation as parts of the whole, but I was brought up short by a question: how did this congregation see itself as a whole? I wondered how this congregation could see itself as the body of Christ without seeing itself as an ordinary body. How could we get beyond what often sounds like pious rhetoric to experience for ourselves the astonishing idea that our particular congregation is the body of Christ?

I decided I would ask them to take a few minutes to imagine their church as a single person and was startled at how powerful this experience was for them and how useful for me as their leader. What I had thought of as a warm-up exercise became the highlight of the day and a lasting reference point for the congregation. Clearly, I was onto something! Over the years, I came to appreciate how critical it is for congregations to have a clear and realistic sense of their identity in order to engage in effective planning. After many experiments with various exercises, I also came to appreciate that the personal identity exercise enables congregations to articulate their identity in a profound and encouraging way.

There were and are other exercises intended to help the congregation gain a sense of identity. Some exercises invite congregations to imagine themselves as an object or animal, for example, "If this congregation were a dog, what kind of dog would it be?" While this is fun and may bring out some useful information, it has no theological or biblical grounding and does not lead to a renewed sense of mission or to effective planning. Another popular exercise has groups write a letter to the angel of their congregation, like the letters to the angels of the churches in the book of Revelation. The problem with this exercise is it tends to encourage participants to make negative judgments about their church. While the angel may be charitable, the "god's-eye view" inevitably sees that the congregation is not all it should be. Of course, no congregation is perfect, but focusing on its limitations and shortcomings is not a good place to start. Congregations beat up on themselves enough as it is. In my experience, the letter from the angel exercise works better when a congregation already has a clear sense of its identity and mission and has the self-confidence to work on problems.

As I said at the beginning of this book, I do not have a definition for congregational identity except for the circular one: "Identity is what makes a congregation unique, distinct from all others." Yet even though the concept of identity is elusive, I find it central to my work with congregations in transition, a category that seems to include almost all congregations these days. Perhaps there never was a time when church life was stable, when most changes happened in an orderly manner, yet we look back nostalgically and seem to see that time stretching out behind us. In those days, drastic change and major upheaval were rare in churches. On the few occasions when there was need for a transitional ministry such as an interim, the aim was to navigate through the change and guide the congregation to a safe harbor of stability once more.

In these days, however, we know that harbors are few and far between, and most of our time is spent in a sea of change. Why are we surprised? After all, individuals in our congregations are frequently challenged in their personal identity as they change jobs and careers, go back to college for retraining, marry outside their social and ethnic group, exit and reenter marriage, blend families, move from one end of the country to the other and back again, live in a constant flood of information they do not know how to interpret, and feel threatened by events and people in countries they never before heard of. This world of constant change is the context of our congregations, and it should not be surprising to us that congregational identity is profoundly affected.

Rural churches have been overwhelmed by the pastoral care needs of farmers and farming communities facing wrenching changes. The industrialization of agriculture has resulted in the loss of family farms and the depopulation of rural areas. At the same time, with the loss of human and financial resources, rural churches are closing or making do with far fewer clergy services. Some rural churches watch with mixed hope and dread as the suburbs of nearby cities eat up farmland and grow closer. Church identities and roles that were once clear have become ambiguous or even irrelevant. What is to become of the rural crossroads church with its cemetery alongside or the small-town church whose town has almost disappeared?

In urban churches, members come and go, leaders move away for new jobs, neighborhoods change drastically, and freeways cut through parish boundaries. Churches no longer know who they are or what they are supposed to do. Identities that once seemed firmly fixed have been revealed as flimsy, too dependent on conventional social frameworks to withstand the waves of change. These days, congregations, like individuals, need to be flexible and adaptable in order to continue their ministry. As with individuals, a deeper and more self-conscious sense of identity is the best preparation for change.

We know that not all churches are flexible and adaptable, however. Some congregations want to be a safe harbor, a refuge from the storms of change "out there." We can understand and even sympathize with their desire: change is stressful, and the people sitting in the pews often need comfort and pastoral care as they struggle to keep up with changes in their workplace, family, and community. More important, churches have a tradition to keep, one that has been handed on from one generation to another and must be faithfully handed on to a new generation. But the gospel comes to us incarnated in forms and languages appropriate to our time and culture, and we tend to confuse these with the gospel itself. Programs, styles of music, the church building—we have seen these features of church life defended with a ferocious determination that suggests they have come to seem matters at the heart of the tradition that must be preserved forever.

I have met many clergy and lay leaders who are bewildered and frustrated by parishioners who have painted themselves into the walls of the church building or who have refused to support a new program designed to appeal to the younger people they say they want to attract. The leaders complain that all the studies were done, the changes were highly reasonable and thoroughly discussed, and all the best change management practices were followed, and still, the congregation voted against the change or sabotaged it with their lack of support. When that kind of resistance happens, instead of resigning in anger, it would be wise for leaders to ask what would make reasonable people who really do love their church behave so irrationally.

My experience tells me that a perceived threat to their sense of identity often lies at the root of the fearful and angry resistance to change. Our parishioners know that buildings and programs are not central matters of faith, but what they feel is entirely different. What they feel is that these things are central to their identity as a church. Threats to identity are perceived to be threats to life itself. Unless the perceived threat to identity is directly addressed, the congregation will continue to resist any change.

What the Personal Identity Exercise Does and How It Works

Leaders can expect three results from doing the personality exercise: an energizing and enjoyable experience for the congregation, a deepened and more realistic sense of congregational identity, and a solid foundation for planning future mission.

The first thing leaders can expect is an energizing and enjoyable experience for the people who do the exercise. This may sound like a rather modest benefit, but few congregations are used to having fun while tackling such a serious question as congregational identity. Congregations in the midst of stressful transitions have often become opinionated, polarized, or conflicted, and an enjoyable experience working together is a real relief.

Most frameworks for discussions of identity require skills that are unfamiliar to all but a few congregants—skills such as analyzing statistics or making abstract statements about general characteristics. Drawing conclusions from charts of statistical information is a learned technique that few people are comfortable with. Trying to identify characteristics of the congregation and state them as a mission statement or core values is an abstract process that many congregations cannot handle well. While these methods may produce results that are quite accurate, they seldom elicit widespread excitement or create the foundation for a common vision.

In contrast, the personal identity exercise elicits creative and playful energies that do not depend on specialists' skills. Imagination, creativity, and humor come out to play when people are invited to picture the church they love as one person. Groups find humorous ways of describing even difficulties and tensions; for example, "she lies about her age." Deeply felt, but hard to describe situations are illuminated with laughter; for example, "perimenopausal." The congregation's affection for its church, with all its foibles and peculiarities, shines through, and even people who are still somewhat caught in old conflicts can engage lightheartedly and respectfully with each other. The energy in the room, along with the noise, always rises through the exercise, and the group leaves with energy left over.

The second and most important result of the exercise is a deepened and more realistic sense of congregational identity. In my experience, few people are convinced of the effectiveness and usefulness of the personal identity exercise until they have experienced it themselves. Congregations and boards I have worked with generally agree to do the exercise thinking that it will be interesting and even fun, but they seldom expect that it will be profoundly important and useful. (I do tell them, but they don't believe me.) What they do not realize is that congregations really do know who they are but have not had a framework or a language to express it. When the congregation is able to articulate its common identity, members have a foundation for a common vision.

The surprise is revealed when the table groups report in. The large group hears a description of what is recognizably the same person from each of the small groups. It is hard to exaggerate the sense of pleasure that fills the room at this point. Affirmation of one's identity is a wonderful experience for a person and equally so for a congregation. Moreover, the personal identity the congregation imagines is always regarded with respect and affection. There is no bad kind of person, no wrong stage of personal life, no useless individual. The image is able to carry the people's sense of problems and limitations within their love for their church. Self-knowledge is a great gift, and self-acceptance is even greater.

The image that is built up by the small groups is recognized as true to life. It takes on authority, real power to shape further thought and imagination. Probably the main reason the image has such power is that it grows from the roots of the congregation, whereas congregational typologies, statistical charts, and other frameworks used to understand congregations are often seen as "outsider" perceptions that cannot possibly contain the uniqueness of our particular congregation. We know that a person is unique and therefore a fitting image for a congregation. The vocabulary of personhood is familiar, thanks to pop psychology, soap operas, and tell-all talk shows. To put it simply, people know about people, at least people in their own social group, and they have a wide range of concepts and a broad vocabulary for articulating this knowledge. While not many are able to analyze statistical tables and see the reality behind them, almost everyone can think imaginatively about ages and stages, life styles and dilemmas and crises of individuals. The language of personhood gives the congregation a way to clearly express what members know about their church. And this particular person has been imagined by them to fit their own reality in their own words. The image rings true.

But is it true? Better, does it lead to a sense of identity that is more realistic than what the congregation had before? In my experience, the answer is yes. Remarkably, even congregations that seem firmly stuck in a false identity are able to "get real" as they work through the personal identity exercise. At least the majority of the people really do know who they are, despite appearances to the contrary. I think greater honesty is possible in the context of the exercise because the members feel in control of the resulting image, and because working on a projected image is less threatening than working directly on their church. Also, even if they have been feeling hopeless about their church, whatever person they imagine always has some hope, a place in God's heart. Even when congregations are suffering from serious problems, there is great relief in expressing the pain. Humor helps, although sorrow is mixed with the laughter. The energy locked up in depression and pretense can be set free for healthier uses, and this person can look to the future.

The third result to be expected from the personal identity exercise is a solid foundation for planning future mission and program. Chapter 5 is all about how to use the image in this way. At this point, we simply note that the particularity of the personal image the congregation develops suggests some futures and precludes others, just as the future of an elderly man is different from that of a young boy, although they are equally valuable and equally called to be faithful in their lives. A widely shared and articulated sense of identity, whatever it is, is the foundation for a common vision, and a common vision is the foundation for effective mission and programs.

When to Use the Personal Identity Exercise (And When Not To)

The personal identity exercise should be used as part of a planning process in the congregation. I have used it in the context of interim ministry, where questions of identity are part of the process. I have also used it as an outside consultant in congregations that are engaged in a review of their mission and structure. The review or planning process might be routine, the sort of exercise every congregation would be wise to undertake every few years, or it might be urgent, imposed by a crisis in the life of a congregation. I suppose the personal identity exercise could be used on its own with no particular goal in mind, but I'm not sure that it would have much more than entertainment value in that case.

There are a few circumstances where the personal identity exercise will not work well.

- Too early in a pastorate
- In the midst of high-level conflict or immediately after trauma
- Too soon after a merger or amalgamation of churches

It is not wise to try to do the personal identity exercise soon after you arrive as the new clergy leader, even though it might seem like a great way to get to know your new congregation. A solid bond of trust is necessary for the exercise to work well. Wait until you have established your pastoral authority and a good working relationship with the lay leadership team. The exercise also requires substantial preparation and that takes time, too. The leadership team needs to gather historical and statistical information, and as many of the congregation as possible need to do some Bible study and theological work.

The richest part of the exercise is the time after the table groups report in, and the leader works with the whole group to build up the image and work on it until it is clearly recognized by the whole group as authentic. For that to happen, the group must trust the leader enough to share even painful feelings, and the leader must be able to draw

on thorough knowledge of the congregation to ask questions that can pull participants to a deeper level. How soon
can you do the exercise? I don't have an absolute answer,
but I need at least six months to get ready. The importance
of the bonding and preparation time is the main reason I
am not as happy with the results of the personal identity
exercise when I do it as an outside consultant. My prefer-
ence now is to work as a coach with the clergy and lay
leadership team, who have built the needed trust and guided
preparations, so they can do the exercise on their own.

It is also not a good idea to try the personal identity
exercise in the midst of heated high-level conflict. The congregation is unlikely to be in a playful, creative mood, and
the exercise (like everything else) will just get sucked into
the conflict and provide ammunition for both sides. The
personal identity exercise is not a conflict resolution tool.
For the same sorts of reasons, it is not wise to do the exercise in the midst of trauma. The congregation is unlikely to
be able to participate freely, and the recent crisis will over-
shadow the results. The exercise is, however, an effective
healing tool once the worst of the trauma has been dealt
with, or the conflict has died down and order has been
restored. The aftermath of conflict and trauma is often a
shaken sense of identity. People are asking, "Who are we,
that we could get so angry with each other?" or, "How will
we continue after this?" In these circumstances, it is a real
gift to be able to work together and affirm the depth of
common identity.

The third situation in which the personal identity exercise is not a good choice is soon after a church merger. It
seems obvious to me now that a recently merged congregation is unlikely to have a clear and common sense of

identity, but I had to learn by experience. I attempted to use the exercise in a congregation formed by a merger three years before our work together and got minimal results. The personal image they came up with was vague and lacked the kind of depth and detail that usually gives the image its authority. I worked hard with the group to try to generate some enthusiasm about their "person" but got nowhere. Finally, I realized that this congregation simply did not have a unified sense of itself. It was still two congregations that were living together, not one congregation.

I have since learned that using the personal identity exercise in merged congregations requires separating them into the founding groups and having each work at its own personal image. Sometimes merged congregations are reluctant to do this—they have worked so hard at coming together that it feels like a betrayal to do anything apart. I persuade them that in order to know and appreciate their roots, it would be good to remember what each church was like. There may also be a significant third group composed of members who have come since the merger and do not really identify with either of the founding churches. They can work on an image of the merged congregation as the only one they know.

Putting the images together involves talking in terms of a marriage or a decision to live together. You can ask how the relationship is going, what's hard and what is fun, what they have learned, and what still needs work. The exercise will allow them to be honest about the circumstances that led to the merger and about the experiences of loss that are always part of mergers. They will also be able to laugh at themselves as newlyweds who get irritated when their new partner doesn't roll the toothpaste tube neatly. As they listen to each other, they may reach a deeper appreciation of the differences between them as both difficulty and gift. The result is a realistic sense of the state of their merger and what needs to be done to keep working together.

Hilltop and Hillside Church (see the introduction to this book) were stuck in a merger that clearly was not working. They found it difficult to face that fact, because they unconsciously believed they must be bad Christians if they couldn't work together—either that, or the other church wasn't really playing fair, or the minister or the judicatory weren't being helpful. When they did the personal identity exercise, they came up with very similar images—both described themselves as feisty old ladies who lived on their own and had no desire to move in with somebody else or to acquire a partner. With that out in the open, they could laugh at themselves and admit that this merger was never going to work, since neither of them was committed to it. The merger had to end.

How long does it take for a merged congregation to develop a single identity? I think it depends on a number of factors. One important factor would be how well prepared the congregations were for the merger: congregations with a firm sense of their own individual identity and realistic objectives for their life together are likely to fare well. Another important factor would be the situation after amalgamation: congregations that are growing gain a new identity sooner, because the new people don't identify with either of the founding churches. A third important factor is the principle of equal losses: if one congregation feels it lost much more than the other in the merger, there is likely to be continuing unhappiness. Badly done mergers can cause pain and trouble for decades. There is a well-known old joke: "We used to have two churches in our town, but then we had church union and now we have three."

Getting Ready to Do the Personal Identity Exercise

Good preparation is the key to good results in the personal identity exercise as in anything else: it is hardly possible to over prepare. The whole congregation and the leadership team need to have clear expectations and a willingness to participate in the exercise, and the event itself should be carefully prepared. I would love to be able to say that I have always done all this preparation, but I know that in the real world it is almost impossible to do everything that follows. What I do know is that the more preparation you can do, the more you will get out of the exercise, and the less you do, the fewer resources you will have to work with the image.

I was asked to come as a consultant to a neighboring church and do the personal identity exercise with its board. This was a large, established suburban church, with many professionals and businesspeople in the congregation. About 30 people gathered with me on a Saturday morning. I began with half an hour of Bible study and then went straight to the exercise. The group, mostly young to middle-aged businessmen, had a little trouble getting into their imagination, but soon they were working away in their small groups. Pulling the image together went quite well. They saw the congregation as a young businessman with a sharp suit, terribly busy.

I realized I was floundering a bit, because I didn't know
what questions to ask, since I didn't know much about the
congregation. Someone said that this businessman carried
an attaché case (this was in the days before Palm Pilots).
This attaché case was a thing of beauty, made of butter-
smooth deep brown leather, so elegant and slim that you
could only put a few files in it—you knew he wasn't the
sort of man who carried his lunch or his gym shoes to work.
The board members went on and on about this wonderful
attaché case. Then one of them said flatly, "But it's a mess
inside, a total mess." The conversation stopped. I knew
something important and true had been said, but I had no
idea what it meant.

We couldn't go any further. I asked what the comment
was about, but they would not tell me, a stranger. All I could
say was something weak like, "I think you are telling me
there is a very serious problem, that everything is not as
smooth and successful as it seems." I left soon after that. I
never did find out what the mess was, and I don't know if
they dealt with it. I learned that evoking such powerful
dynamics without being prepared to work with them was
unfair and perhaps even harmful.

Preparing the Congregation

Preparing the congregation for the personal identity exercise means working on the biblical and theological base of
its commitment to the church. It is impossible to overesti-
mate the importance of this step. In my opinion, we who
are leaders in the church seldom talk about our faith commitment to the institutional church. We should not be surprised, therefore, if most of our congregants have little

ability to think about the church in theological terms. Inevitably, when they search for frameworks to understand the church, they can only use the concepts familiar to them from discussions of other institutions, such as corporations and government. Looking at the church through these frameworks can be valuable; in fact, all sorts of nontheological frameworks are useful. (Indeed, the personal identity exercise uses psychology and other personal language to generate new and deeper understanding.) Yet a church is not a person, a corporation, or a government—it is a church. We have a biblical and theological language that needs to be solidly in place, or these other frameworks are likely to distort the very thing we are trying to understand. Importing concepts such as "customer satisfaction" into congregational studies, for example, may provide us with useful insights, but this concept and others must have clear boundaries set by theological commitments.

The advantage of the personal identity exercise is that it connects quite easily with our biblical and theological tradition through Paul's image of the body of Christ. The ease of that connection, however, is not generally apparent to congregants. In my experience, even with preparation, congregations still find it difficult to hang on to the idea that their church, in all its particularity, is the body of Christ, probably because it is such an unfamiliar way of speaking. Therefore, take time to make it familiar by laying a good foundation before embarking on the personal identity exercise.

Reflect, preach, and pray about the church as the body of Christ. Think about this concept in all its richness as assurance, challenge, and mystery. Most denominations have issued study papers and statements about the church, some of them with substantial theological content. Often congregations are aware of their denominational tradition only as an obstacle, when they find that they can't do what they want to do. But when they study their own denomination's history, decisions, and beliefs about the church, they may come to appreciate their own tradition as a resource, as well as find easier ways to navigate the judicatory's decision-making process. Congregations will also find comfort in the idea that they are not the only ones struggling with church problems and trying to think faithfully about their future. Belonging to a community of congregations is not only a constraint, but a support.

Learn, teach, and preach about the New Testament church. I notice that in many churches where it is not the custom to read all of the lectionary readings for a given Sunday, it is often the epistle reading that gets dropped. When we do that, we miss our best resource for thinking about the church. There are excellent and accessible books and study guides on the New Testament churches and on each of the epistles. For example, the United Methodist Women developed an engaging study on 1 and 2 Corinthians called "Conflict and Community in the Church," which includes not only the study book, but a video and Internet resources.[1] Any congregation doing this kind of study would find that the Christian community's struggles to be faithful in an indifferent or hostile culture are not so new. Paul's letters join us to a community of congregations that reaches all the way back to the first century c.e.

The aim of preparing the congregation is to give members a theological and biblical foundation so they will have a broader appreciation of their congregation. They will continue to ask the questions about problems and personalities, but they will also begin to ask deeper questions about the purpose of their church and how it is growing into the fullness of its status as the body of Christ.

Preparing the Leadership

The leadership team is usually the board of the congregation or the planning committee. They should know the congregation well and have the confidence of the people. They must be committed to helping with the personal identity exercise and following through with an implementation process. Of course, the leadership team will need to do the biblical and theological work along with everyone else. Their special task, besides facilitating the table groups, is to gather and disseminate information about the congregation. Setting out basic information about the congregation sounds as if it would be a simple task, but often it takes a lot of creative work.

Few churches (unfortunately) undertake major review or planning processes just because it is a good thing to do. Most churches feel a need for planning when something is not going well, and some churches wait until there is a crisis before they even think about it. Few congregations have a realistic grasp of trends in their church. For many congregations, their wished-for reality obscures hard facts. I assume congregations that decide to do the personal identity exercise as part of their planning process are experiencing some sort of problem that leads them to suspect that they need to do something different, but I do not assume that they have a clear picture of what is actually going on.

When there is a perceived problem, people are quick to identify the cause and propose a solution; in fact, there are usually several different causes and solutions proposed. The process goes something like this: "There are fewer children in the Sunday school. We are not attracting young parents any more. What we need is a young minister with a family to get the Sunday school going again." Or, "Giving is down. People don't contribute like they used to. We need an every-member stewardship campaign." The step following such a chain of reasoning is often to implement whichever solution gets the most support, and usually the result is disappointing. They get a young minister with a family, but the Sunday school doesn't grow, or they hold a stewardship campaign, but giving continues to decrease. The next step is frustration and blaming: "I told you a young minister wouldn't do it. What we really need is a skilled youth worker . . ." and so it goes. Many churches spend years trying one solution after another and failing, getting more and more demoralized in the process.

What is missing is any analysis of the problem and its context. The leaders need to forget about solutions for the moment and concentrate on describing the problem. They must delve into their own congregation and its history, as well as the community around them, and analyze exactly what is happening to their church. How many children were in the Sunday school in the '50s? Were the parents members of the congregation? Where are those children and their children now? When did the decline start? How has the demographic profile of the neighborhood changed over the same period? Are there young families in the neighborhood now? Are they and their children likely to come and join our church and Sunday school?

By answering these kinds of questions, the leaders begin to get a fuller picture of the problem and realize that solutions are not often obvious or simple. And of course, a similar series of questions must be asked about finances and other parts of the congregation's life. All of this information should be communicated to the congregation in easily digestible bites. It will not make much impact initially, but it will help root the personal identity exercise in reality, and it will certainly support the planning process. Perhaps most important, the leaders and the whole congregation begin to make a shift from being anxious problem-solvers to becoming curious researchers.

The curious researcher stance (a phrase often used in family systems work) cools the emotional temperature of the process. It takes the perceived problem seriously, more seriously than just rushing into a solution, and therefore the people who are anxious about the problem feel they are being taken seriously. It honors the depth of the problem—and the anxiety about it—by searching for the roots of the situation in the congregation's history. Curious researchers find depth and complexity in problems that seemed simple and are able to gently question simplistic solutions by asking what would happen to this or that factor if the proposed solution was implemented. Publishing the research in Sunday bulletins, newsletters, and minutes of meetings tends to arouse lots of interest. Congregations like to read about themselves, and the information begins to percolate through the whole group. When the leadership team members act as curious researchers, they lead the congregation to engage problems at a more sophisticated level without arousing more anxiety and conflict.

The leadership team also needs to be prepared to facilitate the personal identity exercise in their table groups.

You may need to add to the group or select from the group, depending on how many tables you think there will be. Table group leaders need to know the outline of the whole exercise. Their job will be to get the group working on an image and keep them on track. Group leaders should feel free to participate in and contribute to the discussion, but restrain themselves and let others speak first. The leaders many need some coaching in small-group leadership skills.

Preparing for the Event

I assume that congregations all know how to set up large meetings, but some may not be used to working in small groups and will need a little coaching in how to do this. My experience is that you need to have at least four and no more than ten table groups of five to eight members in order to have a productive experience with the personal identity exercise. In family- to pastoral-size congregations, a meeting of the congregation is usually called. In larger churches, the board plus a targeted representative group is usually invited. If you are expecting there will be problems with conflicts or overly dominant voices, do some coaching with the leadership team on group norms and standards before the event. (See appendix 2 for sample handouts.)

Apart from the practical details, the most important thing to prepare is the questionnaire handout for each table. There are some standard questions—age, sex, appearance, health, life setting, recent history—but it is important to ask some questions that grow out of your knowledge of the congregation and some questions just for fun. Here are a few examples of some specific questions:

- What is *Name's* favorite kind of music?
- What does *Name* eat for breakfast?
- What kind of house does *Name* live in?
- What does *Name* do on Friday nights?
- What photos does *Name* carry in his or her wallet?
- If *Name* was given $1000 to spend, what would he or she do with it?

The leadership team's knowledge of the congregation will help to develop appropriate questions.

Another list of questions you may wish to prepare will be the ones you will ask to help the whole group develop the image, so that it takes on the kind of detail and depth that give it authenticity. This part of the exercise requires good thinking-on-your-feet and intuitive skills. If those aren't your strengths, tap the skills of others in your leadership team to help. With the congregation and the leadership as well prepared as possible, all you will need to do is relax and enjoy the process.

Reporting and Follow-up

The first task after the exercise is to report fully and widely to the whole congregation so that the chosen image becomes a familiar reference point to everyone whenever they think about their church. Collect the handouts and chart paper and gather the data together into a typed document. Although this raw data doesn't make very good reading, post it somewhere accessible for everyone to review the details. Next, a good writer needs to take the raw data and write a complete and coherent story of the personal image. (A good example of this kind of report is found at the end of this chapter.) This report will probably be a couple of pages long and should be sent out to the whole congregation. You will also need a one-paragraph description that can easily be inserted in the Sunday bulletin or committee agendas.

It is also important to pay attention to creative unwritten reporting. Find someone who can make a sketch of your person, write a song, or put on a play. Have contests to choose outfits, pick the person's favorite flavor of ice cream—anything at all that will keep the image alive and fresh in the minds of the congregation. Of course, the effort is more intense for the first few months, but it can be valuable to recall the person after some time. I ran across a person who told me that his church still checks up on "Grace" after eight years!

Getting the Word Out

The people of Spencerville-Roebuck Pastoral Charge have been working hard for several years to become healthy and whole so that they can begin a new life. What follows is their report of the personal identity exercise that they did with their minister. This is a fine and very moving example of the honesty and courage congregations can express with the help of the personal image.

> On Saturday, April 9, we held a workshop on church family dynamics. We spent the morning learning about how systems work in families and in the church.
>
> In the afternoon, we had the pleasure of being introduced to Rosebud, who was very open and told us much about herself, her background, her likes and dislikes, her

fears and her joys. She has allowed us to share her story with you today.

Rosebud

Rosebud is a young woman—in her early 20s—who has within the past couple of years moved out of an abusive relationship. This step took no small amount of strength—something that she wasn't aware she had. One day she came to the realization that she didn't like who she had become and knew that she had to make some changes in her life. She searched deep inside of herself and found the insight, the courage, and the faith to take the first step. From that time, she has been on a journey toward self-discovery and healing.

She sees herself filled with inconsistencies as she makes her way day by day through her new life. She is much stronger, though not completely healed. She is dedicated, hardworking, volunteers her time and talents, and very social. Other times, though she isn't proud of it, she can be gossipy, negative, moody, disrespectful, and unfocused. At times she thinks she has come so far in her self-development and then in the next moment, she fears that she is a phony. She remembers what she has gone through and, worried about hurting others, often catches herself in an "addiction to niceness"—worried more about keeping harmony than in making the right choices.

She is grounded in her United Church roots. Her faith is meaningful; her spiritual hunger is profound. She loves Bible study—any search that satisfies her desire for knowledge. She loves children and has a heart for youth. "Feeding" others as well as herself brings joy to her life. She encourages others in their personal journeys and spends much of her precious time volunteering—in numerous ways.

She lives alone in a big, beautiful, old house. She loves it. Unfortunately, she has limited income and is unsure how long she can keep up with all of the maintenance costs.

She is health conscious. She considers herself a homebody and yet somewhat of an explorer. Her tastes are contemporary, and yet she likes to mix in the traditional as she treasures her connectedness with her roots.

She acknowledges the inner tension between her fears and her hopes. In her last relationship, while it was abusive, she was also coddled, stifled, and dependent. As anyone coming out of a relationship like hers, when the going gets tough, she worries about slipping back into her old habits—surrendering to her fear and anxiety, going back to the "comfort" of the past life she knew. But she is careful and determined and recognizes that for her, there is no going back. She is recovering from this past and aches to overcome her insecurities, to find her self-esteem, her independence.

She has stretched herself and is ready to try almost anything. She is daring, fun-loving, adventurous, and charismatic. She enjoys being a little eccentric—just look at her purple hair. How exciting to witness her finding her wings.

She becomes more confident with each step she takes. She has been too hard on herself for far too long. Others appreciate her gifts and her abilities. It has taken her a while to see her true self in the mirror. She is dis-covering who she is—accepting of who she is—and is beginning to like who she is.

Soon, she knows, she will be ready to enter into an-other relationship. She knows what she has to offer and still recognizes her own shortcomings. As she has come to appreciate herself and to believe in herself, she also is better aware of her wants and needs and knows that this awareness can only enhance a relationship.

Her name is a perfect match for her in this place and time. She is a delicate Rosebud, ready to bloom. With all the beauty of the rose, she is fragile—and a little thorny. Handled with care and understanding, envision the joy, the sweet fragrance, and the pleasure she offers as she blossoms.

5

What Does "Someone Like Us" Do?

After the congregation has developed a personal identity and the image is familiar to everyone, the next question is, What can, should, and will we do? Knowing who you are does not tell you exactly what you should do, but it does indicate a range of realistic and unrealistic options. With Paul, we are working on the assumption that each congregation is the body of Christ just as it is and that it has all the gifts it needs, and needs all the gifts it has, to be a faithful incarnation of God's work in the world. If we believe in God's goodness and kindness, we must believe that the ministry God has for us is one for which we are suited. God does not ask the frail elderly to run marathons or teenagers to run large corporations. Our ministry will certainly be challenging; indeed, the Gospel promises it will take all that we have. But the Gospel also promises that whatever we have will be enough.

As the congregation considers its mission, the personal identity becomes both a generator of ideas and a criterion for evaluation. Whether the church is in good shape or in a life-or-death crisis, a firm and realistic sense of who they are will help the members make better choices. In this chapter, we will be looking at some specific examples of how the personal identity image supports planning for mission and program. We will also consider how other types of resources and exercises can be brought into the picture.

Age and Gender

Congregations are usually clear about the age of their personal identity image. Occasionally they have a struggle admitting the real situation (see the story of Dublin Street Church at the end of chapter 3), but the group as a whole is able to identify the truth. When I first began using this exercise 20 years ago, the gender was also clear. Now I find that many congregations no longer have a definite sense of what male and female congregations look like and choose a somewhat androgynous image. In theory, male congregations emphasize programs and activities, while female congregations emphasize relationships. Changes in the society at large have made these stereotypes less useful.

The age and gender of the person is not primarily the average of the congregation, although a congregation with a majority of young families and children is not likely to identify itself as elderly, and a congregation with a large majority of women is not likely to identify itself as male. The age and gender of the personal image come from common ideas about how teenage boys or middle-aged men or elderly women behave. These common ideas are, naturally, stereotypes, and that is why they work. The congregation will choose from among images that it knows, and the image will be meaningful to members. It is important to ask the question, "What is it like to be an 80-year-old woman?" (or whatever image they have presented) so people can articulate the meanings contained in the image. Interestingly, the exercise works well in different cultural contexts, since the content of the age/gender image is not given by the exercise, but by the participants. For instance, being an elderly woman in a culture that honors and cherishes its elders is very different from being an elderly woman in a culture that considers them useless or problems. The congregation's members will tell you what it means to them, which is what matters.

Once the members are clear about what it means to them to be a certain age, it is good to bring in material on the life cycle of congregations and the ages and stages of life in congregations. There are many good articles and books on these subjects and they will provide new dimensions to the conversation.[1] Generally, three ages stand out as important for mission planning—youth, middle age, and old age. Having said that, all ages present characteristic challenges and opportunities that should be explored.

Youth

Congregations that see themselves as under 18, like South Valley Church (see the end of chapter 2), find that thinking seriously about their age allows them to focus their considerable energies while paying attention to their need for structural support. South Valley made three important decisions that were directly based on its sense of being a

13-year-old boy. First, members decided that "Eddie" should not take on the organization and management of a food bank and clothing depot. Eddie would not do well at a long-term management task; instead, he should do short-term, high-energy projects. Second, they decided that the part-time church secretary should become a full-time church administrator, so that routine tasks such as production and distribution of minutes, coordination of building use, and planning for meetings would be done for Eddie. The third decision was that when it came time to look for a new minister, they would look for a mature person with solid experience. They felt that Eddie needed firm, almost parental leadership.

None of these decisions would have been made without the guiding image of 13-year-old Eddie. Yet together they freed the young congregation to do many short-term outreach and study projects. There was enough structure in place that congregational life never fell into total chaos, and yet there was a joyful sense of spontaneity in worship and program that kept attracting young couples with young children. As the surrounding suburb matured, so did the congregation. Eddie grew up. Twenty years later, South Valley is no longer Eddie, but middle-aged Sally!

Middle Age

Being 50 (the exact number is arbitrary) represents middle age, the time when people are at a high level of maturity and energy and can work most effectively. It is also the time of midlife crisis, menopause, children leaving home, and being closer to the end of life than to the beginning.

Churches that place themselves in this age group often feel bored or restless and sense that change is coming or is already happening, yet they feel stuck. They can drift for years in this state until something upsets the equilibrium. Any kind of problem, even quite a minor one, can reveal a disturbing state of stagnation.

St. Mark's Church (see chapter 3) is an example of such a congregation. One good thing that came out of members' problems with clergy leadership was a thorough review of the congregation's identity, vision, and mission. Without such a crisis, they might have drifted for years. The key comment about "Debra" was, "You need to really stop and think about your future. Lots of women get scared and jump too fast into a new relationship or a new job without really thinking about what they need and can do."

Middle-aged congregations, like individuals, are at the peak of their mature power and identity. They can renew their vision and passion and use their gifts for a new emphasis on serving the community around them as they continue to grow in faith. Or they may enter a period of decline and denial if they do not adapt to this stage of life. If they are unwilling to face the challenges and opportunities of middle age, they may behave erratically, looking for a magic solution that will return them to an earlier stage. They may look for a "trophy minister" or embark on poorly conceived programs that fail and leave them feeling confused and ashamed.

The antidote to making a fool of yourself in midlife crisis is self-knowledge, and that can only be achieved by the hard work of realistic reflection on who you are at this stage in your life.

Months after St. Mark's did the personal
identity exercise and developed the image of Debra, Rev.
Bill overheard a conversation between two members. One
said, "Well, I think all we need is a young minister with a
family who will attract young families again." The other
member laughed and said, "Debra would never go for someone like that!" Bill smiled with satisfaction. The personal
image was working just the way it should. Also, the two
members had just given him a great idea for the next annual meeting.

At the meeting, Bill had the congregation sit in table
groups once more. He led the whole group in remember-
ing Debra, and then he invited each table to have some fun
and "help the search committee" by writing a personal ad
for Debra. He handed out some personal ads from the news-
paper as examples. With much laughter, the tables set to
work and then shared their ads with the whole group. The
results appeared in a new personals column in the next
newsletter.

Pretty, Witty & Gritty
SWF, NS, 45, indepen-
dent, health con-
scious, loves fam-
ily life, outdoors
and music. SEEKING
someone of like in-
terests, self-assured,
fun loving, musical.
Must love children of
all ages. Honesty and
integrity a must.
Must be of age. OB-
JECT friendship &
possible long-term
relationship. Will
train to suit.

Ready Again
Musical, fun-loving
single w kids, casual
& competent. SEEK-
ING caring & com-
passionate person
ready for commit-
ment. Must be stable
& dependable, good
communicator, good
sense of humor, will-
ing to learn. Good
singing voice desir-
able. Needs healthy
appetite. OBJECT
meaningful long-
term relationship.

Desperately Seeking
Let me show you
love and the way!
Pleasantly mature,
music-loving, full-
figured. Financially
secure with good
house. SEEKING ma-
ture, caring, sponta-
neous & passion-
ate person. Needs
healthy appetite.
OBJECT long-term,
spiritually enriching
relationship.

The personal ads were a great way to remind the congregation who they were as a middle-aged congregation and the kind of clergy leadership they needed for the future.

Old Age

Congregations that see themselves as a person over 75 experience themselves as elderly. Being elderly involves inevitable losses—loss of ability and mobility, loss of status and social power. For many elderly people, illness threatens, and aches and pains are constant reminders of limitations. The end of life is in sight, and thoughts of death are common and appropriate. For individuals, these difficult aspects of aging can be balanced by the love and respect of family and community, the many programs and activities designed especially for seniors, the satisfactions of a life well lived, and faith in God's continuing care after death.

For elderly congregations, however, growing old can seem like unrelieved loss. Elderly congregations generally see themselves as shameful failures rather than as honored elders. Other congregations, even ones in their own denomination, are seldom helpful. They tend to see the elderly congregation as a problem church and confirm the sense of failure. "Successful churches" have young people, youth groups, and lively Sunday schools. Elderly congregations are thus unsuccessful, and someone must be to blame. The burden of guilt is often too heavy to bear, and elderly congregations become anxious and deny their reality (see the story of St. Paul's in chapter 1). They become angry with themselves, their leaders, and their denomination as they try to find someone to blame. The elderly congregation may become like an embittered old person, obviously in trouble, yet difficult to love and impossible to help. At this stage, the congregation is really unattractive, and the cycle of guilt and blame is intensified. Outsiders look on in judgment and say, "No wonder no one wants to go there."

The personal identity exercise is wonderfully useful in helping elderly congregations regain their self-respect. Identifying themselves as elderly allows them to face their reality in a good-humored way. After all, growing old is no one's "fault"—it's a normal part of life! For congregations also, growing old is not likely anyone's fault. Probably there were some decisions made in the past that the members wish they had made differently, but likely they were reasonable decisions made in good faith. In my experience, the only factor to blame is demographics and social change. Rural depopulation, changing ethnic composition of neighborhoods, and rising housing costs lead to neighborhoods with fewer young families. In these circumstances, it is normal for congregations to grow old. Elderly congregations begin to gain energy as they let go of paralyzing guilt and glimpse their reality as the body of Christ.

The personal identity exercise also challenges elderly congregations to see themselves as still part of God's work in the world. Fortunately, elderly congregations usually have lots of members who are aging with grace and dignity, despite the inevitable limitations and losses. And often these members have a strong, mature faith and a commitment to prayer and practice. They understand perfectly on an individual level that God does not love them less or expect less commitment from them just because they are 80 or 90. Although they cannot do what they once could, they are still hard workers to the limit of their abilities. They pray faithfully, read their Bible, and visit the sick, at least by phone. As long as they are able, they attend worship, prepare and serve food, and give generously. If an elderly congregation can begin to imagine itself as one of these great older people, still called to be the body of Christ, then they are well on their way to imagining new mission.

The exact shape of that mission depends on the gifts of their particular body. Some elderly churches have seen that ministry with seniors is their calling because they live in a retirement area. Churches have built seniors' residences or nursing homes on their property and searched for younger, active seniors (rather than young families with children) to be the leaders of this ministry. Some elderly churches have had to face the reality that their church will die. The focus then shifts to faithful death—making a "good will," celebrating the faithful ministry of the past, and praying for resurrection. Elderly churches are almost always candidates for redevelopment, rather than renewal or revitalization.[2] The problem of course is that elderly congregations by definition almost always lack the gifts needed for redeveloping themselves. If redevelopment is to happen, the congregation must envision the change and then invite others to take over the resources and control the process. The judicatory can play a key role at this point, making sure the elderly congregation is honored and cared for while a new ministry is developed. It is surely not easy to let your church go into someone else's hands, but it is not impossible, either.

A congregation in much the same situation

as Hilltop Church (see the introduction to this book) saw itself as an elderly woman named Ellie. In the past, it had been a neighborhood, family church, never very large, but always somehow managing to make ends meet, usually by sharing a minister with another congregation. The people had a fine, independent spirit and many gifts, including a remarkable gift for hospitality. Newcomers were genuinely welcomed, but there were only a few of them each year—not enough to make up for the older members who died or moved away. The finances were precarious and the congregation clearly could not survive more than a few years. What should Ellie do?

After considering various options, including closing or simply carrying on until they went broke, the congregation made a bold choice. It was true their neighborhood no longer had many young families they could hope to attract, but there were many students living in apartments and basement suites. Ellie decided to reorient herself toward the people who worked and studied at the nearby university and lived in the neighborhood. This kind of ministry would probably never be self-supporting, but the congregation could support it by renting its second building to another church. The congregation agreed to contribute its property, buildings, and money, as well as its prayers and hospitality. Members asked the judicatory to help them find some of the skilled people needed to manage the project. A full-time minister was appointed for three years to work half-time on the campus and half-time in the congregation. Ellie embarked on an entirely new course. What if the judicatory didn't deliver the promised help? What if the congregation couldn't raise enough money from renting its buildings to carry on? They would run out of money in a few years. Ellie was anxious, as well as excited. Still, she decided she'd rather go out in style than just drift away. She is a very fine and faithful old lady!

Fitness

Questions about fitness and health in the personal identity exercise usually elicit clear responses. Comments about fitness are related to how the congregation perceives its energy and effectiveness in ministry. Unfortunately, congregations often do not give themselves enough credit for their ability to minister well. They may have inappropriate ideas about what a good level of fitness would look like for them. They forget that fitness is different at each stage of life and in different circumstances. Both a 90-year-old and a 19-year-old can be fit in their own way, and a person recovering from a serious accident will not (yet) be as fit as before the accident. Congregations can use their personal identity image to set realistic fitness goals for themselves. Developing fitness programs for congregations, which can be seen as renewal strategies, requires attention to the realities of their particular situation.

Debra, the image created by St. Mark's Church,
was described as having the following state of health and fitness:

- Has recovered from a period of stress and depression
- Generally in good health, although needs to continue to work on fitness
- Needs to think about her spiritual health
- Needs to take care of herself (and make time to eat a proper breakfast!)

When board members considered this description, they recognized its accuracy. St. Mark's was a busy church with a remarkable number of programs and activities for a small congregation. It seemed that the members would gather to help a cause, celebrate a liturgical season, or just have fun at least once a month. Weekly programs filled the calendar throughout the year, and committee meetings took up any spare time. Some members spent two or three nights a week at the church, plus a couple of Saturdays a month and, of course, Sundays. The board members thought that all this activity was the equivalent of high physical fitness in an individual.

The area of spiritual fitness seemed more problematic. As the board members thought about Debra, they could see a number of places where issues of spiritual fitness came up. Debra was overly busy—she didn't even have time to eat a proper breakfast—and she was concerned about the balance of work and family time. But what about personal time for herself? No wonder she recognized a need to think about her spiritual health!

The board members were full of suggestions on how to tackle the problem. "We could have a special worship service and Bible study on Wednesday nights," one member said. "We could have a book club and meet for breakfast on Sunday morning before church," someone else suggested. "I hear St. Anne's had a wonderful series on contemplative prayer last year," another commented. "Whoa!" said Rev. Bill. "Time for a reality check—how many of you came to the Wednesday evenings in Lent last year?" Only two or three hands went up. "Simon," Bill said, "I don't want to put you on the spot, but why didn't you come?" Simon said apologetically, "I wanted to, but you know I have the board or a committee meeting on Tuesdays, and choir practice on Thursdays. I just couldn't face another weeknight out." "Exactly," Bill said. "We are already very busy. Another series of activities and programs is not likely to work very well."

Everyone paused to reflect. "Do we need to drop some of our activities?" Simon asked. A lively discussion followed that question, but there was no consensus on what could or should be eliminated. Harry mumbled, "Maybe we're just not very spiritual." Brian said, "Maybe spiritual fitness is not really about doing more or different activities at all. It could be more about *how* we do everything, rather than *what* we do." This was a long speech for Brian, and everyone looked at him with interest. "I mean, could we be more spiritual in our board meetings?" he asked. "It seems to me that we ought to give some leadership. I mean, we are supposed to be leaders."

The board members looked a bit uneasy at the idea of being spiritual leaders, but Bill reminded them that they really couldn't expect Debra to take spiritual fitness seriously if the board wasn't willing to put some effort into it. He offered to find some articles to help them explore how they could grow as spiritual leaders and circulate them before the next meeting. With that, the meeting adjourned.

Health

The personal identity exercise sometimes reveals congregational problems in images of disease or injury. When a congregation describes itself, even in a joking kind of way, as unwell and unable to function appropriately for its age, the pain is real and should be treated seriously. Congregations in such painful circumstances need to be assured that they are still the body of Christ, that they have not lost their identity as a church, and that they can recover from an illness or injury and offer any permanent scars to God as part of their identity. In my experience, congregations rarely describe themselves as sick, but when they do, it is out of immediate and disabling pain. Injury is an easier image to accept, although they usually cannot speak freely about it except as a past event. They describe themselves as recovering or healed from a health crisis of some kind. It is important to probe into such a statement to articulate what the present state really is.

Illness

Being sick or having a disease is an uncomfortable image because it describes a systemic, internal problem. Systemic thinking is still not a commonly available skill, although it is proving to be useful in working with congregations and other organizations. Congregations may be able to tell the story of a repeating pattern without seeing a system. Linear thinkers want to trace cause and effect and thus be able to lay blame. (It is easier to think of yourself as a victim of someone else's actions than as part of a sick system!) Systems thinkers must practice the difficult discipline of accepting responsibility without worrying about blame. Naming a systemic problem requires taking responsibility for an internal problem that has become part of the congregation's life.

Shady Glen is a large, busy church in a prosperous and stable suburb. The high cost of homes in the area means that there are fewer young families than there used to be, yet the congregation still has a variety of age groups and a full range of programs. Shady Glen has had multiple staff for decades and paid them well. They have always had a senior minister who was a fine preacher and pastor, an assistant minister who oversaw programs for youth and families, a Sunday school coordinator, an office administrator, musicians, and a pastoral care visitor. With so many staff, it wasn't surprising that they always seemed to be hiring or saying good-bye to someone. However, when Amy was elected chair of the personnel committee, she became concerned as she reviewed the files.

She saw a remarkable amount of turnover, especially among the clergy staff. At the first meeting she chaired, Amy suggested they talk about the personnel history of Shady Glen in the past 20 years. She explained that she had noticed reports of conflicts between the staff and the congregation and observed that the clergy, all of whom were well qualified and carefully chosen, stayed only four to six years, which seemed a rather short time. "You know the old saying," she remarked. "Once is an accident; twice is a coincidence; three times is a pattern. There is a pattern of poor relationships with the clergy that results in their leaving suddenly and unhappily or even being pressured to resign."

The older members on the committee were shocked and defensive, even though Amy had kept her tone neutral. They remembered each of the ministers in the past 20 years, and they didn't see a pattern. "I know we've had five associate pastors in that time, but they're all young fellows who want churches of their own," said one. "Pastor Helen wasn't a fellow, and she wasn't so young," objected another. "She hated to leave, and we were really sorry to lose her." "Oh, she couldn't get along with Rev. Washington," the first one said. "No one could get along with Rev.

Washington," another quipped. "That's not true, you know," another said. "He was unpopular with a certain group that made it their business to get rid of him." "Yeah," commented another old-timer, "the same group that gossiped and griped about Rev. McDougal." "But that group was all gone by the time Rev. White and Rev. Mercer were here, and they were unhappy and left, too. Remember all those nasty letters?" someone added. Amy let all the stories come out, prompting only when they forgot or tried to gloss over the facts.

After an hour of this, the personnel committee members looked at each other. They had to admit that Amy could be right. It did seem that their pastors had not been happy at Shady Glen. "I guess we haven't been doing a very good job," one of them said gloomily. "That's not the point," Amy replied. "I think the whole congregation is involved in the pattern. It's like an infection, something toxic—it seems to spread on its own. The point is, we don't want it to happen again. We have already had complaints about Rev. Deutsch and Rev. Jackson from a few people. Can we handle these issues so that the story will end a different way this time?" Everyone agreed, but no one knew how to proceed. Amy suggested they invite the judicatory personnel officer to come and advise them as soon as possible, and the committee accepted her proposal with relief.

Injury

Injury is common in the image resulting from the personal identity exercise. Congregations, like individuals, experience various traumas and crises that leave them in pain and unable to function as well as they expect, at least for a time. The sudden death of the pastor, vandalism in the sanctuary, a betrayal of trust by a leader, a fire in the church, a serious conflict—any of these may appear in the history of the personal image as car accidents, falls, muggings, or other common experiences of trauma. The trauma affects some members more than others, of course, and leaders arc usually aware of individual pastoral needs, but the congregation as a whole is also injured and needs pastoral care.[3] The personal identity exercise is useful in identifying and caring for the congregational level of the trauma.

The image of injury should be taken seriously and explored with regard to its immediate and long-term effects on the person of the congregation. Congregations often minimize the effects of injury, but the image helps them articulate their shock, pain, anger, and depression in healthy and appropriate ways.

Blue Valley Church went through a year of

turmoil over its denomination's proposal to ordain openly homosexual people. Fortunately, they had a good minister, and the discussions were civil, but feelings ran high on both sides. During the turmoil, a number of people left, just to escape the unpleasantness. When the congregation finally voted with a large majority to endorse the proposal, several long-time members and key leaders left to join another denomination. The minister, feeling bruised by all the conflict, resigned. Overall, Blue Valley lost almost a quarter of its congregation and its minister.

A year later, as the congregation struggled to live into its new situation, the interim minister, Rev. Mary, led them in the personal identity exercise. Members' image of Blue Valley was a man named Matthew, about 35 years old, married, with a large multigenerational family. Matthew was a professional—perhaps a teacher, social worker, or civil servant. He was an urban-hip kind of guy with a diverse group of friends and was progressive in his thinking. He was kind and thoughtful, trying to do his best for his family, his work, and his community. And he was a war veteran and had had a leg amputated. This shocking last comment was presented by one table group and greeted with stunned silence and then slow nods all around the room.

When Mary worked with them to build up the image, she asked about this terrible injury. She decided to take a matter-of-fact tone and asked, "Was it an above-the-knee or a below-the-knee amputation?" Someone with a young nephew who had an above-the-knee amputation explained that this was much more disabling than the below-the-knee kind. The whole group mulled this over and decided that Matthew's was a below-the-knee amputation. He was somewhat disabled but able to walk well and live normally. Some of the group said that, in fact, he was fully healed and should just get on with things. But Mary kept working the image. This was the best conversation Blue Valley had had about its situation all year.

"What's it like, one year after having your leg amputated?" she asked. "It hurts," someone said grimly, "and it's going to hurt for a long time." "For sure," another said, "but it doesn't hurt as bad as it did at first." "There's that thing called phantom limb pain," someone else said. "You can still feel the missing parts." Everyone groaned in agreement. Someone added, "People don't understand that you can't do everything you used to do, at least not as well." But another countered, "Yet Matthew doesn't need to be treated as if he is totally incapable, either. Personally, I think he's about ready to put his handicapped parking pass in the glove compartment." The congregation applauded, and with that hopeful image they moved on.

Mary was so grateful for this conversation. The congregation had acknowledged the depth of its pain and distress at the loss of so many members and yet could see that it was making progress in a healing. They were still somewhat handicapped but were feeling almost ready to accept the reality of their life and think of what their mission should be now. She thought, in the mysteries of grace, Matthew might grow a new lower leg and foot eventually, and his terrible injury could become an old war story.

Failure to deal seriously and appropriately with the injury can result in the institutional equivalent of unacknowledged post-traumatic stress disorder. Sometimes we see bizarre behavior and peculiar structural arrangements that are attempts to protect injuries from long ago.

St. Luke's Church was a pleasant small-town

church that had a long history of not keeping its clergy more than five or six years. The judicatory found the turnover difficult to understand, because St. Luke's seemed to be the kind of church that would encourage long pastorates. As yet another minister resigned to accept a call elsewhere, the chair of the board asked the judicatory for help in figuring out what was causing the ministers to leave. So Rev. Carol Head arranged to interview all the former St. Luke's ministers she could find. The results were intriguing.

The former ministers and, even more, their spouses remembered St. Luke's and its town fondly. They had all started out with the vision of a long, satisfying pastorate in a town where their children would grow up happily. Their decision to leave came much sooner than they had expected. Many of these ministers had gone on to successful pastorates of 10 years or more. Why had they left St. Luke's? It was hard to pin down the specifics, but a pattern began to emerge. The ministers had indeed been unhappy and the issue was usually around money.

Carol already suspected the truth, although it took a while to track it down. She found the answer as she talked with a congregational member whose father had been the chair of the board in the 1950s. He remembered overhearing his father talk about it. Apparently the minister at the time was stealing money from the benevolent fund. It wasn't a lot of money, a few hundred dollars over several years, but it was shocking nonetheless. The chair of the finance committee confronted the minister with the evidence and he confessed. The whole thing was hushed up (although the story did leak out rather widely). The minister resigned and went to another church. The chair of the finance committee resolved that such a thing would never happen again at St. Luke's and instituted a system of rigorous controls that included requisitions and receipts for any expense, no matter how small, and never allowed discretionary spending by the minister or any other staff. Fifty years later, all of the actors in this drama were long gone, but the cumbersome financial controls remained.

The present chair of the board was shocked and somewhat suspicious when he read Carol's report. "But we've always been proud of our high standards with money! Strong control protects everybody, doesn't it?" Carol agreed, but pointed out that it was possible to go overboard in this, as in all things. What their former ministers felt was that St. Luke's treated them as if they were dishonest, likely to steal any money they could get their hands on. St. Luke's needed to trust its clergy, to treat them like equal partners rather than irresponsible children. Carol thought that if the board heard the story in full, they would probably understand that they were distorting their church's life because of a problem that had only occurred once, 50 years ago.

Character and Present Circumstances

The present context of the congregation includes much more than age and health. Character and present circumstances are what give depth and particularity to the personal image. For a congregation, as for an individual, age and health are very important factors, but other factors will be equally important in determining how the congregation copes and what its possibilities are.

We often see individuals behave differently in what seem to be similar situations. Two elderly women, both in good health for their age, are no longer able to live alone in the large houses they have owned for decades. Both experience profound grief as they ponder what to do. One gets her family to help her choose a good assisted living residence. She is sad, but she makes a determined effort to decorate her room with some precious things, to keep in touch with old friends, and to engage with the people at the residence. She settles into her new home quite quickly and enjoys the social activities. The other woman refuses to move and gets her family to help her stay in her house. Her children are worried about her, and there are many

little and not so little accidents and falls. They and she
know that one day, she will likely fall down the stairs and
break a hip, if not her neck. She will likely end up in a hos-
pital and never come home. That's the way she wants it.

We have probably all seen both these stories acted out
by individuals and by congregations. What makes the difference? For the two elderly women, it is some combina-
tion of character (internal factors) and circumstance
(external factors) that leads them to act in such different
ways. Congregations also have something analogous to
character, and certainly they have external circumstances.

Internal Factors

Congregations have something like a personality, which can
also be called the organizational culture. This culture is
shaped by a great variety of factors. Certainly, history plays
a large part. For instance, St. Luke's Church (see above)
was rigidly controlling about financial matters to protect
itself from being hurt again. But one might also ask, was
there some predisposition to react that way 50 years ago
when the system was instituted? Besides the particular
history of the congregation, there is the general history of
the social setting. The concept of generational cohorts[4] can
be used to illuminate this factor. If the St. Luke's board and
its treasurer were of the generation that grew up in the
1920s, came to adulthood in the '30s, and served in the
armed forces in World War II, their tendency to extreme
caution about money matters may be partly explained.

History alone, however, does not account for all the
particularity of the congregational culture. Influential leaders can shift the whole system for entirely personal rea-

sons and put in place new behaviors that quickly become "the way we have always done it." Perhaps the treasurer at St. Luke's had a dark history of stealing money and used the church system to fight his own demons. There could be many explanations, which makes it rather clear that explaining the culture may not always be useful. It has its uses when, as at St. Luke's, a congregation persistently engages in behavior that is not only unproductive, but actually harmful. In those circumstances, discovering when and why the behavior began may free the congregation to choose something different. But it may not.

Changing the cultural system of a congregation, like changing the character of an individual, requires self-knowledge and disciplined hard work. Any system seeks to maintain itself, and when it is disturbed, it tries to return to its former stable state.[5] Changing your character requires gaining perspective on yourself, so you can think clearly about what you are doing. You also need a strong sense of identity in order to work through the discomfort that change brings without feeling totally threatened. Congregations working at cultural change require the same sort of tools—the personal identity exercise is helpful in this process. The personal image is a projection of the congregation's identity and is easier to think about than the amorphous thing called culture. The well-articulated sense of identity that results from the exercise can give members the strength to change part of that identity. In my experience, congregations find it relatively easy and even fun to talk about the character of their personal image, including eccentricities and problems. They can go on to imagine a course of "therapy" that would lead to changes.

Rev. Carol Head was surprised to get another call from the chair of the board at St. Luke's. She was even more surprised to hear that the board and the treasurer had decided not to change their finance policy. "We thought about it, truly we did," the board chair assured her, "but we really can't see how any reasonable and honest person could object to careful money management. After all, you folks at the judicatory office are always telling us to be more careful about handling money. And your stewardship person often tells other congregations what good managers we are here at St. Luke's." Carol responded cautiously, "But your practices do seem to cause some problems for your clergy." "Well, maybe so," he responded, "but ministers have no call to be spending church money anyway. We decided we just need to explain the policy to the new minister and make sure he knows how it works, and everything will be okay. Thanks for your help, Reverend. It was really interesting to hear about that minister 50 years ago. I can really see why we set up our policy."

Carol didn't know whether to laugh or bang her head against the wall. Both seemed appropriate! She wandered down the hall to share the story with her colleague, Jim. They laughed together, and then Jim said, "You know, this strict money management has become part of St. Luke's culture, and they will not change it easily. To you, it is clear that the policy is harmful, but to them it has positive value. Even the evidence you think counts against it just confirms that they are right. "I can see I was a little naive," Carol said, "thinking that I could find a simple cause-and-effect type solution. But I think they will still have problems with their clergy, and the issues may run deeper than this stuff about money management. That comment about ministers having no call to spend church money made me wonder if St. Luke's treats its clergy like irresponsible children in other ways, too." "Could be," said Jim. "Anyway, there's nothing more we can do about it except keep an eye on the situation." Carol still fretted. "I just wish I'd done a better job with them." "Don't be hard on yourself." Jim said. "You have taken the first and most important step in systemic change; you made them conscious. You made them think about what they are doing. So far, they are just resisting the knowledge you gave them, and trying to fit it into the existing system. But the conversation won't stop there. I wouldn't be surprised to hear from St. Luke's again in a few months, this time asking for help with change."

External Factors

It may seem too obvious to mention, but external factors influence how congregations behave. It is not too obvious, because congregations and leaders often forget this wisdom. It is true that patterns often go unnoticed (like the pattern of unhappy ministers at Shady Glen Church, above), but it is also true that sometimes "three times *is* just an accident." Events that happen at the same time become connected in our mind. You get out of bed and step in something nasty the cat did on the rug; you spill coffee on your last clean shirt; the car won't start; and you conclude this morning is jinxed! Of course, each of these events is unconnected, except in time (synchronicity), but at an emotional level, they add up to a pattern. After this kind of start to the day, we are likely to be out of sorts, wondering what's going to happen next. We are likely to overreact, even to a small additional incident.

Congregations can also have the same sort of experience. St. Mark's Church (see chapter 3) had two unfortunate experiences in a row with its ministers, with one divorcing shortly after leaving and the other being removed for health reasons. These troubles had little or nothing to do with St. Mark's action or inaction, but of course they affected the congregation profoundly. There was no connection between the two events, and the congregation was no more likely now than before to experience such problems again. Even though it was unreasonable, however, they felt anxious about calling their next minister. They were worried the same thing would happen again.

Bad things—and good things—happen to congregations, sometimes in series, without much rhyme or reason. The results can be disconcerting. A new minister arriving in a congregation that has had several bad experiences with clergy may find the people unwilling to trust and bond with him or her. The new minister may feel a great deal of anxiety in the air and may be the recipient of unresolved feelings of anger and hurt. The new minister is likely to feel confused and hurt, even if he or she knows the history. Again, the personal identity exercise will give a way to work through these problems in an appropriate way.

Rev. Bill Thompson was getting ready to

leave St. Mark's. The search committee had called its new minister, Rev. Edith Goldman, who would be arriving in six weeks. On Sunday, after church, the congregation met to talk about how they wanted to welcome her. They talked of calendars of events and housing help and who would be available to orient her over the summer and help her kids get registered for school. Someone said they wanted to do everything right and added, "We don't want any problems this time." The level of anxiety in the room rose suddenly.

Bill reminded them of Debra and asked them to think about what she needed to do to welcome the new minister. "She needs to let go of the past and welcome Rev. Edith with an open heart," one of the members said. "She has to keep reminding herself that Rev. Edith is not Matt, and she's not Dorothy," another said. "Or Bill!" another interjected. "Debra should tell her story to Rev. Edith and explain that if she seems to be reacting to someone else, Edith should call her on it," Simon said. "But we don't want to rehash all that old stuff," someone objected. "Of course not," Simon replied. "I just meant we should be open with her about our feelings and how we might slip into old ways occasionally." The whole group thought Simon's approach was the right one.

With that done, the congregation sent Bill home, so they could plan his farewell party.

Epilogue

The good news for congregations remains, "You are the body of Christ." That is still the most astonishing, the most heartening, the most challenging fact I know about each and every congregation. Indeed, it is the *only* thing I know about all congregations. The personal identity exercise is intended to flesh out the body of Christ, to help congregations know who they really are at the most profound level of their being. Of course, sometimes congregations don't want to delve that deeply. Sometimes congregations are so pleased and fascinated with their personal image that they do not complete the process by identifying their image as the body of Christ. It is understandable that congregations that feel wounded or uncertain—a great many congregations—need some time to savor the healing effects of articulating and affirming their identity. Nevertheless, congregational identity can become a narcissistic trap if the identity does not become the foundation for a sense of mission as the body of Christ.

When a congregation sees itself as Eddie (or Debra or Ellie), the body of Christ, the members feel both encouraged and challenged, and the Spirit may lead to some amazing places. A church is not, after all, a person. A human body cannot become young again, cannot give itself away and still live, cannot die and live again—at least not in the world as we know it. But a spiritual body, the body of the risen Christ, may and does do these things. Indeed, this last impossibility, bringing new life out of death, is something of a Christian specialty, and should not surprise us, although it does every time.

Rev. Sue Alexander (see chapter 1) looked around the table with astonished gratitude. This was the first meeting of the board since the whole congregation had done the personal identity exercise, and the change was like a breath of spring after a long winter. She along with Beth and Fred had decided to hold the board meeting after church on Sunday and to invite anyone who wanted to continue the discussions about "Pauline" and her future. There were actually a dozen people, twice the usual number. What is more, they were talking eagerly with each other.

Beth called on Eleanor, a retired school principal, to read the description of Pauline. Eleanor had volunteered to take all the documentations from the exercise and write a coherent account of St. Paul's personal image, and she had done a really good job. Everyone listened intently.

> Pauline is an older woman with many hidden qualities. She tries to dress well, although she doesn't much like the fashions nowadays and says you just can't find good

quality anymore. Strangers may see her as just a boring old lady, but they don't know how much she has contributed to the community in the past and how much she does, even now.

Pauline was a stay-at-home mom who was led by her Christian faith to volunteer thousands of hours helping her community be a healthy, beautiful, and interesting place to live. She was always especially devoted to children and families, and for many years all the children in the neighborhood came to her house for milk and cookies and a hug. She has many skills and a wide network of acquaintances in the community, although a lot of friends have moved away or died in recent years. Her own children have moved away as well, and she doesn't see them as often as she would like. To tell the truth, she is lonely now.

Pauline's health is pretty good "for an old lady," as she says. She stays as active as she can, but she knows her hearing is getting worse, and there are days when she is very stiff. Sometimes she is irritable and not the nicest person to be around. She has not had any major health problems yet, but she is worried about how complicated everything is now that she has limited energy.

She is frightened when she sees so many of her contemporaries dying, or worse, moving to nursing homes. She desperately wants to keep her independence, to stay in her own home—"they can carry me out feet first," she says. On her worst days she thinks she will just rent out the basement and hope for the best. After all, she won't last many more years.

But on her better days, Pauline knows she can trust God, even in this new and difficult stage of her life, and even beyond life. Surely God isn't finished with her yet, even though she is elderly and unhappy. There must be something she can contribute.

Eleanor sat down, and looked anxiously at the solemn faces around the table. Finally, Beth said, "It's a great report, Eleanor. It's just what we said, and it's all true." Sue could feel a cloud of depression descending again. It was time to move on. "What can Pauline do? What are her options? Last week, we thought of these:

- "'Go to a nursing home' means close the church; join other congregations.
- 'Rent out the basement and hope for the best' means carry on as we are as long as we can, cutting expenses as much as possible, and renting out space to produce income.
- 'Contribute' means find a new mission for Pauline."

The only other suggestion, from one elderly lady, was that St. Paul's should call a young minister with a family who would bring back the young people. Sue swallowed hard and asked politely what that would look like in terms of Pauline. Fred piped up, "Get married to a 20-year-old hunk and start a new family!" Everyone roared with laughter, even the woman who had made the suggestion. They decided that the three ideas from last week were the real options, although there could be a number of ways of doing them. And there was no doubt in their minds that a new mission was the way they wanted to go, but what could it be? What could God be expecting of Pauline?

Every idea they thought of seemed to require more people, more money, more energy than Pauline had. They began to grow sad again: it seemed they had failed, that they had waited too long. Sue reminded them: "You are the body of Christ. You have all the gifts you need to be the body of Christ just as you are. The question is, what are the gifts you have, and what are the needs they fit?"

They kept coming back to the building and the vast church experience of the congregational members: these were the gifts Pauline had to offer. Then someone mentioned an article in the denominational paper a few months ago that talked about ethnic congregations and their problems getting established. The article said these congregations often didn't have good worship space, and they needed help finding their way around the culture and the denomination's systems and structures. "There's a mission for us right there," said Eleanor. "We have the gifts—a building and all our experience. They need space and the support of experienced church members. What if we could find a congregation that would move here and take over the building and become a new St. Paul's?"

Excitement—and fear—flickered through the room. "But what about us?" one of the elderly members said. "If we give the building to them, will we still be able to worship in English? Will someone look after us?" Sue said, "That's a good question, and there will be many more important issues to work on—and pray about. But if Pauline's gifts are fully used in mission, we can trust in God's care. And, most important, the body of Christ will be here, in a new manifestation!"

The rest of the meeting buzzed with energy as the board drew up lists of people to contact with questions that needed to be answered. Sue closed with prayers for Pauline, for her past ministry and her future, and for the church known as yet only to God, the one Pauline would become.

Death and Resurrection at Willingdon Heights

St. Paul's is a fictional church, as I said at the start of this book, but I know a real congregation that is quite similar, Willingdon Heights United Church in Burnaby, British Columbia. "Willie," as she was called, is now a multiethnic congregation. The pastor is Korean, and most of the congregants are Korean and Phillipino. They worship in English, so the old congregation didn't have to move down to the basement, which was a grace they hadn't expected. Willingdon Heights is just beginning this journey into a new identity and a new mission. Who knows where it will end up?

All this is happening because a rather difficult old lady named Willie came to see that she was the body of Christ. She saw that her calling, her gift, and her mission was to die so that another very different life could grow. Willie is no more: she is among the saints, one of the great cloud of witnesses, and the body of Christ rejoices.

Appendix A

Workshop
Outline

1. Time will vary: Bible study and worship appropriate to the occasion and congregation. The focus is on the congregation as the body of Christ.

2. 20–30 min: Explain what it means to imagine a congregation as a person. Tell three or four stories of congregations' personal identity images; choose stories different from each other and different from the present congregation.

3. 5–10 min: Hand out the worksheet and explain the details of the process. Draw attention to group norms as necessary (see appendix B).

4. 20–30 min: Table groups work at the task. Leadership team members keep the groups on track and make sure good process is followed. The presenting leader

may circulate and coach any table groups that have trouble getting started.

5. 20–60 min: (Time will vary depending on the number of table groups.) Table groups report to the whole group. The presenting leader keeps the process moving, allowing each report equal time. Key elements are written on chart paper and posted on the walls.

6. 20–30 min: Presenting leader works with the whole group to create the composite image out of the table group reports. More detail is added and critical features and issues are identified.

7. 10 min: Explain briefly how the image will be used. Close with prayers for the "person."

Appendix B

Sample Worksheet

Imagine our church as a single person. Think of the stories you just heard—how is our church different from those churches? Use the questions below to help you describe our church—use the spaces on the sheet or the back of the sheet to record your thoughts. There is no right answer and it doesn't matter whether you get to all of the questions. You will have 25 minutes to work together, and then a member of your group will tell the whole group what you have written down. Have fun!

We imagine our church as a person . . .

1. Which gender?

2. About how old?

3. What does he/she look like? (general appearance, style, clothes)

4. What does he/she do? (occupation, lifestyle, hobbies)

5. What is his/her state of health and fitness?

6. What is his/her life setting? (recent events, new challenges, opportunities)

7. What is his/her favorite TV show and radio station?

8. What does he/she eat for breakfast?

Additional questions might relate to the particular circumstances of the congregation (see chapter 4 for suggestions).

Reminder

- Our meeting is a sacred space, where respect for the gifts of others is generously given and the movement of God's Spirit is invoked and expected.
- Everyone has a chance to speak, though not every thought has to be expressed.
- All views and opinions are received with respect, but not necessarily with agreement.
- When one is speaking, the others grant them appropriate time and space.
- Everyone shares responsibility for making our experience enlivening and enjoyable.

Notes

Chapter 1
A Case of Mistaken Identity

1. Usually attributed to Tom DeMarco, software engineer and organizational change consultant.

Chapter 2
You Are the Body of Christ

1. The Nicene Creed.
2. A Google search gives about 40,000 references.
3. Nineteenth-century hymn by Charlotte Elliott.

Chapter 3
Who Are We Really?

1. "The Living Church" words: Art Allen. Music: "Father Abraham" (traditional)

   The living church has many parts;
   Many parts make up Christ's body;

I am one of them and so are you;
So let's all do our part.   *right arm*
left eye
right foot

Repeat, adding a new movement each time, until everyone collapses in general hilarity.

Chapter 4
Exploring the Personal Identity Exercise

1. J. Shannon Clarkson, ed., *Conflict and Community in the Corinthian Church* (Nashville: United Methodist Church, 2000).
2. Report of the personal identity exercise at Spencerville-Roebuck Pastoral Charge, a two-point charge of the United Church of Canada in Eastern Ontario. Used with permission.

Chapter 5
What Does "Someone Like Us" Do?

1. A good place to start would be the article by Martin Saarinen, "The Life Cycle of a Congregation." Available on the Alban Institute Web site, www.alban.org.
2. For a brief introduction to the concepts of renewal, revitalization, and redevelopment, see "What Does Our Congregation Need?" by Kathryn Palen in *Alban Weekly,* March 14, 2005, available at www.alban.org/weekly/2005/050314_CongNeeds.asp. The article also mentions additional resources.
3. General strategies on ministering to a traumatized congregation can be found in Jill M. Hudson, *Congregational*

Trauma: Caring, Coping, and Learning (Herndon, Va.: Alban Institute, 1998).

4. A good overview of this subject is found in Carl G. Eeman, *Generations of Faith: a Congregational Atlas* (Herndon, Va.: Alban Institute, 2003).

5. These are key concepts from family systems theory, an invaluable resource for understanding the cultural system of a congregation. A good basic introduction is found in George Parsons and Speed B. Leas, *Understanding your Congregation as a System* (Herndon, Va.: Alban Institute, 1993).